THE SAMUEL AND ALTHEA STROUM LECTURES
IN JEWISH STUDIES

THE SAMUEL AND ALTHEA STROUM LECTURES
IN JEWISH STUDIES

*The Yiddish Art Song,*
performed by Leon Lishner, basso,
and Lazar Weiner, piano
(stereophonic record album)

*The Holocaust in Historical Perspective,*
by Yehuda Bauer

*Zakhor: Jewish History and Jewish Memory,*
by Yosef Hayim Yerushalmi

*Jewish Mysticism and Jewish Ethics,*
by Joseph Dan

*The Invention of Hebrew Prose:*
*Modern Fiction and the Language of Realism,*
by Robert Alter

# The Invention
# of Hebrew Prose

*Modern Fiction
and the
Language of Realism*

ROBERT ALTER

UNIVERSITY OF WASHINGTON PRESS

*Seattle and London*

*Library of Congress Cataloging-in-Publication Data*

Alter, Robert.
  The invention of Hebrew prose.
  (The Samuel and Althea Stroum lectures in Jewish studies)
  Bibliography: p.
  Includes index.
    1. Hebrew fiction—History and criticism. 2. Realism in
literature.  I. Title.  II. Series.
  PJ5029.A47  1988    892.4'35'0912    87-37181
  ISBN 0-295-96622-X

For my mother
TILLIE ZIMMERMAN ALTER
(1903–1987)
in loving memory

# Contents

INTRODUCTION
1

1. FROM PASTICHE TO *NUSAKH*
15

2. TOWARD A LANGUAGE OF EXPERIENCE
43

3. REALISM WITHOUT VERNACULAR
69

EPILOGUE: LANGUAGE AND LITERARY REALISM
97

NOTES
111

INDEX
117

# Acknowledgments

This study, in a somewhat shorter form, was first presented as the Samuel and Althea Stroum Lectures at the University of Washington in the spring of 1987. I would like to express my gratitude to the Jewish Studies Program at the University of Washington and to its director, Hillel Kieval, for inviting me to give the Stroum Lectures and for the warm hospitality extended to me during my stay in Seattle. The manuscript benefited palpably from the close reading it was given by my friend and colleague, Chana Kronfeld. I have learned much from her suggestions, including the ones I decided to resist. I am grateful to Janet Livingstone for her meticulous preparation of the typescript. It has been a pleasure to work with Naomi Pascal, editor-in-chief of the University of Washington Press, and with my manuscript editor, Gretchen Swanzey. A sabbatical salary supplement from the Humanities Research Council of the University of California at Berkeley made it possible for me to take off a semester during which I prepared these lectures. Typing costs and incidental research expenses were covered by special funds provided by the chancellor of the University of California at Berkeley. Finally, I want to express my appreciation for my alert students in a Berkeley graduate seminar on Hebrew stylistics in the fall of 1985, where the idea for this book initially took shape.

# Introduction

The story of modern Hebrew literature in Europe is both intriguing in itself and generally instructive about the surprising possibilities of literary expression; but, given the paucity of translations and of critical studies in Western languages, it is scarcely known outside the circle of readers of Hebrew. This is hardly the place to undertake a concise history of modern Hebrew literature, but before approaching the prose fiction writers who will be our concern, it may be helpful to establish some general notion of where this literature came from and what were the circumstances under which it operated. I will not offer a detailed catalogue of places, names, and dates but rather a sketch of the historical milieu in which, against all odds, Hebrew literature by the end of the nineteenth century came to flourish.

The newness of modern Hebrew literature has long been a subject of debate among Hebrew literary historians because the supposed emergence of the modern movement in eighteenth-century Germany was preceded by eight continuous centuries of secular belletristic writing in Hebrew, first in Spain, then in Italy and northern Europe. (I will have a bit more to say about these antecedents in my first chapter.) This premodern tradition was at first wholly restricted to poetry and remained preponderantly poetic, though it did develop a genre of mosaic narrative in rhyming prose and also, in the Renaissance, some closet drama. But the new movement that surfaced in Enlightenment Germany was, I think, different in kind from its predecessor because of its fundamentally ideological character.[1] That is to say, by the late eighteenth century European Jewry was launching on that process of radical historical transformation we call modernization, and what was at issue now in the act of writing Hebrew was not just an aesthetic pursuit but a programmatic renegotiation of the terms of Jewish collective identity. It is surely not a coincidence that Christian Wilhelm von Dohm brought out his essay, "Concerning the Amelioration of the Civil Status of the Jews" in 1781, that Joseph II of Austria issued his Edict of Toleration in 1782, and that the founding journal of the Haskalah, or Hebrew Enlightenment, the quarterly *HaMe'asef,* began publication in Koenigsberg in 1783. The Haskalah as a coherent movement would last a full century, until the trauma of the pogroms of 1881 made its rationalist meliorism untenable for most Hebrew writers, who then turned to nationalist and neo-Romantic literary trends. In its first decades, didactic essays and almost equally didactic poetry predominated, the writers being preoccupied with how to reform Jewish education, Jewish social conditions, and Jewish theology. The first instances of prose fiction, which began to appear around 1820, were lampoons of Hasidic obscurantism and so partook of the general reformist impulse.

By this time, the Hebrew movement had moved eastward from its original centers in Berlin and Koenigsberg to Vienna, as the rapid progress of assimilation in Prussia eroded the base of Hebrew readers there. Though Vienna itself may be a "Central" European city, its Jewish hinterland, we should remember, was Polish Galicia, also part of the Austro-Hungarian empire, down to the First World War. Here and elsewhere, Hebrew literature was associated with the great movement of Jewish migration from the small towns, or *shtetlach,* to the cities that continued through much of the nineteenth century on into the early decades of the twentieth century. (One might recall, as notable instances of the general trend, that Jakob Freud and Hermann Kafka migrated from their native *shtetlach* to Vienna and Prague, respectively, thus making possible the future careers of their illustrious sons.) Soon there were centers of Haskalah activity in Galicia itself, in Brody, Tarnopol, Lemberg, and Cracow; and by 1840 the new Hebrew literature had also put down roots in Lithuania and in Russia proper, where it was destined to attain its greatest achievements.

As I have suggested, prose fiction was long a peripheral genre in the Haskalah: the first Hebrew novel does not appear until 1853, and an artistically mature body of fiction, free of didactic insistence and stylistically adequate to its subjects, does not begin to emerge until the 1880s. This emergence will be the subject of my first chapter. But I would note here that the eventual embracing of the novel form may well be another manifestation of the substantive newness of modern Hebrew literature in comparison with earlier phases of secular literature in Hebrew. The novel's generic project of comprehensive realism, of making language effect a sovereign illusion of reality, set if off from earlier genres. To write, let us say, a sonnet or a poetic epigram in Hebrew was an act of competitive cultural imitation, but one carried out within the confines of a highly conventionalized formal structure, and, as such, chiefly an aesthetic exercise, however deep the feeling behind some of the individual poems. To write a novel in Hebrew, on the other hand, was to constitute a whole world in a language not actually spoken in the real-life equivalent of that world, yet treated by the writer as if it were really spoken, as if a persuasive illusion of reality could be conveyed through a purely literary language. It was, as I shall try to explain in the course of this study, to enter deeply into the mind-set of European culture with a thoroughness not characteristic of premodern Hebrew literature; it was to invent a new secular Hebrew cultural identity as if it were somehow, uncannily, native to the European sphere.

Who were the people who created this new literature? How did they get a knowledge of the language sufficient to such an undertaking? What were the material conditions in which a literature so anomalous sustained itself? The makers of modern Hebrew literature were, almost without exception, male and the products of an Orthodox upbringing. (In the earlier Haskalah, a good many still preserved some form of enlightened Orthodoxy; later on, the overwhelming majority of the writers were men who had broken decisively with their childhood world of Jewish observance.) The gender and the religious background of the writers were determined by the peculiar educational system developed by European Jewry before its entry into modernity; the system, in turn, was associated with the equally peculiar social structure of eastern European Jewry; and both require a little explanation.

One of the oddest—and most crucial—cultural circumstances of traditional eastern European Jewry is that its masses, by and large, lived under the conditions of an impoverished peasantry while enjoying almost universal literacy. They were not, of course, a peasantry permitted to work the land: for the most part, they eked out their living as middlemen, petty tradesmen (and often, indeed, tradeswomen), peddlers, estate managers and tax collectors, artisans. But a typical *shtetl* house, as one can see from photographs and films taken in Poland as late as the 1920s, looked not very different from the makeshift quarters of a black sharecropper in the American South: a one-room shack with dirt floor, without plumbing, crowded by a family with many children, perhaps even with the addition of an old grandparent. One readily understands why Mendele Mokher Sefarim, the greatest fictional chronicler of these Jews in the Russian Pale of Settlement, called one of his typical towns *Kabtsiel* ("Beggarsville").

I have said that these near-paupers and paupers were mostly literate, but it was a two-track literacy reflecting a two-track educational system. The girls did not attend school but were instructed at home to read the vernacular Yiddish. Since the Hebrew prayerbook was written in the same Hebrew alphabet as Yiddish, grown women thus educated could fulfill the impulse of piety and "read" the prayers, but without understanding more than isolated words and phrases. The boys began *kheyder,* or elementary school, before the age of five and were immersed in a curriculum that was entirely limited to the close study of Hebrew and, later, Aramaic texts.

The method of instruction would hardly seem conducive to fluency in Hebrew. The young boys were led through the text of the Pentateuch verse by verse, each Hebrew phrase being given its Yiddish equivalent in a kind of oral interlinear translation. Other books of the Bible might be accorded some attention in preparation for their public reading at the appointed festivals (Song of Songs at Passover, Ruth at Shavuot, and so forth), and biblical texts fixed in the daily prayers, including dozens of Psalms, would be learned by heart through sheer force of repeated recitation. But there would be no formal teaching of principles of grammar, no vocabulary lists, no exercises in composition. Indeed, the teenage students who happened to get hold of a Hebrew grammar treated it pretty much as underground literature, knowing that their rabbinical mentors would regard as an act of subversion any attempt to study the Holy Tongue systematically, with "secular" tools, as though it were a language just like any other.

By the time a boy reached the age of legal induction into Jewish manhood at thirteen—if he had been an alert pupil and if his schoolmaster had not been totally incompetent (incompetence being more or less endemic to the system)—he could read biblical Hebrew with an approximation of understanding. He would have had some introduction to the primary rabbinic text, the Mishnah, and to the main medieval Hebrew commentaries on the Pentateuch, and would have gained some comprehension of the Hebrew of the prayerbook. But in fact, the extreme unevenness of instruction meant that most products of the *kheyder* were functionally illiterate in Hebrew, retaining only the most rudimentary vocabulary and a fuzzy or mangled understanding of particular texts.

After the age of thirteen, a large part of the student body dropped out—some after a year or more of additional instruction—to become apprentices, to assist in the family business, or otherwise to enter the work force, and sometimes to be married off by their parents by the time they were fifteen. The more gifted went on to the *yeshivah,* or talmudic academy, often having to move to a larger town where there was such an institution. The subject of study at the *yeshivah* was exclusively the Babylonian Talmud, a vast corpus of texts composed in a mélange of Hebrew and its cognate language, Aramaic; as always, the language of discussion among students, and between students and teacher, was Yiddish. The schooldays were long, the demands relentless; students worked in pairs over the difficult texts and their commentaries and then listened to a general lesson from the *yeshivah* instructor. The complementary intellectual qualities they were encouraged to develop were a prodigious retention by heart of the talmudic texts and their biblical precedents (*beqi'ut*) and an analytic sharpness accompanied by ingenuity (*ḥarifut*). Most boys left the *yeshivah* by their late teens, some, having received ordination, to take up rabbinical posts, many, having entered into an arranged marriage, to enjoy a period of private learning subsidized by a prosperous father-in-law who was willing to pay this price in order to have his daughter married to a man of learning.

From the account I have offered, it must surely seem a mystery that anyone could have emerged from this educational system with a sufficient grasp of the Hebrew language to write an essay, a travel book, a sonnet, or, especially, a novel. The *yeshivah* population was the intellectual elite of central and eastern European premodern Jewry. The Hebrew writers produced by the *yeshivot* were an elite within an elite. In part, I mean simply that they were the equivalent of the A+ students in the system, and certainly the evidence many of them offer of retentive memory and (to a lesser degree) of dialectic subtlety, *beqi'ut* and *ḥarifut,* is formidable. But I am also referring to a special mental aptitude, not necessarily valued within the system but abundantly useful outside the system—an aptitude the Germans call *Sprachgefühl*—an innate sense, like perfect pitch in music, for how language should properly sound, joined with a relish for the sonorities and the semantic colorations of Hebrew words in their classical idiomatic combinations.

Minds of this almost preternaturally prehensile cast would catch onto every nuanced collocation, every linguistic particle, in a traditional Hebrew text, both those that were part of the curriculum and those that were not. And as a new Hebrew culture began to shimmer before such unusual students as a radical alternative of Jewish identity to that of the Orthodox system, they would, even in the *yeshivah* milieu, do a good deal of reaching, often surreptitiously, beyond the curriculum—to the parts of the Bible not officially studied, to the medieval philosophers and poets, to those newfangled Hebrew grammars, and, worst of all, to the godless journals, the poetry and fiction, of the new Hebrew literature. Even a moderately receptive yeshivah student, who had stayed within the confines of the talmudic curriculum, would have been able by the age of eighteen to compose certain limited kinds of Hebrew texts—say, a florid prose letter to a future bride (to be translated to her) using a pastiche of biblical phrases, or an opinion on a question of talmudic law using a more businesslike rabbinic Hebrew with an admixture of Aramaic. But the elite of the elite, those prehensile minds I have described, having used the system against itself, would be able by the same age to produce in Hebrew a piece of popular science, a critical essay, a long poem in hexameters, or a work of fiction. This was not a language anyone was speaking, certainly not in the nineteenth century. But out of a comprehensive familiarity with the large body of traditional Hebrew texts, biblical and postbiblical, and counting on an audience whose intimate acquaintance with this corpus matched their own, these young men could compose quite freely in Hebrew. To compose well, making the language address modern predicaments persuasively, was another matter: how the trailblazers learned to do this will be the subject of the chapters that follow.

The class background of the Hebrew writers is elusive. It is sometimes said that they derived chiefly from the merchant class—Ezra Spicehandler, for example, suggests that in the early nineteenth century the great trade fair at Leipzig was a center of transmission of the German Haskalah to the East through the contacts there between merchants from Prussia and from Polish Galicia.[2] But "merchant" may be a little misleading, because in Jewish society it embraced everything from prosperous fur traders and timber dealers to people who maintained wretched little stands in the streets for the sale of odds and ends. The writers came as frequently from the bottom rungs as from the top of the mercantile hierarchy, and so they can scarcely be said to represent an economically privileged class. Although, in a typical poor family, an adolescent son would be expected to help support the household by working full-time, this was, after all, a society that placed immense value on learning, and in which learning was a means of social ascent; so when a boy showed signs of intellectual gifts by the age of thirteen, great efforts would be made to enable him to continue his studies, poverty notwithstanding. Given the talmudic route to Hebrew literacy, no doubt reinforced by a certain genetic background of intellectual aptitude, it is not surprising that a good many of the Hebrew writers had fathers who were members of the rabbinic intelligentsia—*yeshivah* instructors or even *yeshivah* directors, local rabbis, ritual slaughterers (a function that required talmudic learning), or independent scholars of Jewish law.

The one social class drastically underrepresented among Hebrew writers was the new Jewish urban proletariat that had formed in the industrializing cities of central and eastern Europe by the latter part of the nineteenth century. Perhaps this was because this class had been more rapidly removed from the sources of rabbinic learning than any other in Jewish society. In any case, when members of the Jewish proletariat thought about a programmatic renegotiation of the terms of collective existence, it was typically through socialism, and the language used was the language of the Jewish masses, Yiddish. Although it is true that Yiddish and Hebrew during this period were cognate literatures, and although many of the important writers actually produced work in both languages, only Yiddish evinced a general association with the values and aspirations of the urban proletariat. A surprisingly small proportion of the Hebrew writers were born in the large cities. For the most part, they ended up in the cities, where they sought modern culture, freedom from the restrictions of Orthodox society, and a sustaining coterie of like-minded secularist Hebrew littérateurs. Their writing, however, often concentrated on their native *shtetl* world or, alternately, on the deracination of the Jewish intellectual displaced from the *shtetl* and struggling to find himself in the anonymity of the modern city.

It is hard to imagine how these men, impelled by the quixotic vision of creating a new secular literature out of a sacred language, managed to sustain themselves, not to speak of how they managed to sustain their common enterprise. Serving as Hebrew tutors to the sons and daughters of affluent Jewish families in the cities was one characteristic means of meager support. Some earned a living as editors, correspondents, or even typesetters in whatever existed in the way of Hebrew journalism (more of which in a moment). Although most of them were autodidacts, some managed to obtain university degrees, usually by migrating from Russia, where they were excluded by the *numerus clausus,* to Germany or Switzerland, and a few were able to practice one of the trained professions. By and large, the economic circumstances of Hebrew in Europe were unbroken hard-luck stories; their sheer persistence in their literary enterprise bore witness to their fierce commitment to the idea of creating a modern literature in Hebrew.

We do not have precise data on the numerical size of this movement, but it could never have been very large. As I have intimated, the chief defining focus of the Hebrew revival was the literary periodical, from eighteenth-century Koenigsberg to twentieth-century Odessa and Warsaw. The circulation of most of these would not have exceeded that of a highly specialized American scholarly journal. The pioneer publication, *HaMe'asef,* probably had no more than 1,000 subscribers at the outset; by the time it was faltering, in 1797, it had only 120 subscribers, and yet it managed to limp on, appearing sporadically, for another twenty-two years, still thought of in Haskalah circles to the east as an important source of ideas and literary models. The Hebrew journals were often quarterlies, sometimes monthlies; *HaYom,* the first Hebrew daily, was issued in Petersburg in 1886. Toward the end of the nineteenth century, *HaTsefirah,* for a while also published as a daily, sold in Russia as many as 15,000 copies per issue. This was in all likelihood the outer limit for circulation of anything published in Hebrew. The typical journal would have had no more than 2,000 subscribers, and most volumes of fiction or poetry would have had printings of the same magnitude, occasionally a little larger, often even smaller. If we add to our calculations the probable circumstance that copies of journals and books would have been shared by several readers, it is still unlikely that most works published in Hebrew in the nineteenth and early twentieth centuries were actually read by more than 10,000 people.

Why, then, would anyone have chosen to pursue literary ambitions under such difficult conditions? The writers were not free of moments of despair: a famous case in point is the poem "For Whom Do I Labor?" (*"Lemi 'ani 'amel"*), in which Y. L. Gordon, the major poet of the Russian Haskalah, imagines himself the last of the Hebrew bards as his audience disappears into the vistas of assimilation. There was, to begin with, a negative reason for the fidelity to Hebrew: most of the writers had taught themselves Russian, or German, or Polish in adolescence or after and did not have sufficient mastery of the language of the general culture to write in it. Yiddish, of course, had always remained an alternative; but in the minds of many of the writers it was associated with a culture they sought to transcend, a culture that lacked prestige.

To restate this attitude in positive terms, Yiddish, even when it was felt by writers to have the intimate appeal of a native language rich in colloquial nuance, could not offer a whole set of values that was associated with Hebrew as the classical language of Jewish culture. There was, first of all, the far from inconsequential matter of historical longevity. Only Hebrew spanned more than three millennia of national experience and had been used by Jews in all the far-flung regions of the Diaspora. Only Hebrew was associated with Jewish political autonomy, and the awareness of this association played a crucial role in Hebrew literature long before, and beyond, the emergence of political Zionism. For if Jews were to create a culture like others, not dominated by a clerical establishment and not defined exclusively in religious terms, the great historical model had been cast in Hebrew on the soil of ancient Palestine. The biblical texts, moreover, in their sublime poetry and their brilliant narratives, had a literary cachet for which Yiddish could offer no equivalent.

Ultimately, it seems to me that the passionate commitment to Hebrew was impelled in shifting proportions by both aesthetic and historical-ideological motives. On the aesthetic side, Hebrew had always been the most valued language of Jewish culture, if not the most commonly used in everyday life, and had long been the medium of refined literary exercises and epistolary art. With a certain aestheticization of Jewish culture, symptomatic of modernity, this attitude toward the language became for some a kind of addiction to its beauties, even to its purely formal properties: one relished a well-turned Hebrew phrase, an elegant Hebrew sentence, as elsewhere one might relish Mozart or Cimarosa. The abiding delights of this aesthetic addiction could not be replaced for our writers by any other language, not even by their native tongue. At the same time, many of the writers had a compelling awareness that this language was not only beautiful but timeless—a consideration usually powerful enough to outweigh whatever anxiety they might have felt about the tininess of their audiences. As S. Y. Agnon, a writer closer to our time but deriving from this central European milieu before the First World War, once observed of his own classicizing style: "My language [is] a simple, easy language, the language of all the generations before us and of all the generations to come."[3] Though few Hebrew writers would have stated matters so flatly, in such a provocatively false-naive manner ("a simple, easy language"), Agnon's assertion expresses a fundamental feeling shared by many about the historical role of the language.

In sum, the creators of modern Hebrew literature in Europe were impelled by a sense that the language through which they sought to shape a new Jewish culture had a unique aesthetic dignity and a unique historical resonance. This sense sustained them in the shabbiest material circumstances, when there was barely a readership to address, when the culture to come was represented here and now only by the handful of literary colleagues with whom they fraternized and with whom they collaborated on the new Hebrew journals and publishing houses. But even the most ardent loyalty to the language as a repository of distinctive values could not conceal the awkwardness and the artificiality of classical Hebrew as a medium for the representation of modern realities, whether social, historical, relational, or psychological. What was needed to make Hebrew transcend these inadequacies was the bold intervention of genius, which would find ways to make the old language answer to a radically new world. In the chapters that follow, we will observe three decisive moments in that process of creative intervention.

# 1
## From
## Pastiche
## to
## *Nusakh*

The fashioning of a living Hebrew prose as an instrument of realistic fiction is one of the most astonishing chapters of modern literary history. It was carried out on European soil, before the revival of Hebrew as a spoken language, by a handful of daft elitists, with scant encouragement and only the most threadbare means of material support, writing for barely visible audiences. The first Hebrew novel did not appear until 1853. This was a full century after the new literary movement known as the *Haskalah*—a term meaning both to possess understanding and to impart it to others—had been launched in Prussia by the circle of Moses Mendelssohn, in emulation of the rationalist, cosmopolitan, and sublime-aesthetic values of the European Enlightenment.

The earliest Hebrew novels were didactic, technically awkward, and stylistically wooden; but, quite implausibly, by the 1890s fiction of eccentric genius was being produced in Hebrew, and a decade later there were subtly persuasive expressions of psychological realism that seemed perfectly comfortable with the nuanced modulations of style of European modernism. This literary revolution was brought about by writers whose native language was Yiddish; whose general reading—for the most part, autodidactic—was in Russian, occasionally in German; and who would not even have agreed altogether on how to pronounce the texts they produced. Their unlikely success at inventing Hebrew narrative prose before there was spoken Hebrew offers striking evidence of the powers of cultural renewal latent in the Jewish people on the brink of modernity and also raises instructive questions about certain received notions concerning the roots of the mimetic language of the novel in ordinary speech.

Language will be our concern throughout these considerations, and so we will need to have some sense at the outset of the historical peculiarity of Hebrew. Let me stress what every student of Hebrew literature or Jewish history recognizes as the most self-evident fact—that Hebrew in the two thousand years of its dispersal was never a dead language. It had ceased to be a vernacular, with the exception of certain regional pockets, in ancient Palestine by the time of Jesus, but for the next two millennia it continued to serve a variety of literary uses, both sacred and profane, and to develop through time, absorbing foreign influences, changing structurally, and expanding lexically. The most clear-cut continuity was in poetry. From the seventh century to early modern times, liturgical Hebrew verse in a wide variety of forms was composed in Palestine, Iraq, Yemen, North Africa, Spain, Italy, France, and elsewhere and was regularly used in the synagogue. Toward the end of the tenth century in Andalusia, a new secular poetry, at first self-consciously emulating Arabic models, began a rich literary tradition that was carried on and modified from Spain, Portugal, and the Provence to Italy and Holland as late as the eighteenth century.[1] The one form of belletristic narrative prose in this tradition, the *maqama,* an itinerant frame-story composed in rhymed prose with verse insets, was really an adjunct to poetry and would offer no real precedent for modern fiction, apart from a rare episodic borrowing by later writers for comic-grotesque passages. Over the centuries, Hebrew prose carried out other tasks—as the vehicle for devotional tracts, for philosophy (most conspicuously, when the works of the great medieval Jewish philosophers were translated from Judeo-Arabic into Hebrew as the Jews migrated or were driven from Arabic-speaking Iberia), for chronicles, community records, legal discourse, biblical exegesis, wills, international commercial correspondence, and so forth. Only a language of abundant resources could have conducted all this varied business for more than fifteen hundred years. It was, nevertheless, a very different order of business from that of a nineteenth-century novelist describing the nervous flirtation between future lovers, or a fat man trying to button his overcoat in a pelting rainstorm, or the look of an urban landscape enshrouded in fog. The would-be Hebrew novelist a century ago had inherited a language that was lively and various, but not lively and various to his specific purposes.

The rise of the novel in eighteenth-century England offers, at least on the surface, a perfect counter-example to the linguistic peculiarity of Hebrew. The English novel could not have happened, literary historians have long contended, without the famous rise of the middle classes. It was their plainspun, mercantile idiom, according to one familiar account, that displaced the rhetorically ostentatious and more Latinate language of the writers who had received traditional schooling; it was their language that became the norm of the new genre, the formal guarantor of its authentic representation of reality. By this late point in the history of criticism, we are all aware that any literary use of language is an artifice, that the notion of a transparently referential language is a will-o'-the-wisp. But it is plausible enough that the illusion of transparency effected by the first English realists was nourished by the way they could draw on the colloquial, hitherto subliterary traits of the ordinary spoken language of their time. This is the argument made by Hugh Kenner in a suggestive essay, "The Politics of the Plain Style."[2] From an early moment in the period of emergent realism, he quotes a 1667 text by Bishop Thomas Sprat commending "a close, naked, natural way of speaking," which is precisely to the stylistic point of the new genre. Such a way of speaking in print, Kenner proposes, generates trust in the reader, however undeserved, that the truth is being told. This trust makes possible the enterprise of realism.

What, then, was the aspiring Hebrew realist to do? He had no "naked, natural way of speaking" to imitate, no living language of merchants and artisans but, on the contrary, only a heavily layered language associated with figures whom Bishop Sprat might well have denounced as mere wits and scholars. I refer, of course, to pervasive questions of diction, tone, idiom, rhythm, and syntax, setting aside the immense but more mechanical challenge faced by Hebrew writers a hundred years ago in simply having the words to say *pocket watch, railroad station, cigarette,* or *samovar.* To gauge the difficulties facing the Hebrew novelist in the latter half of the nineteenth century, one must imagine Defoe trying to write *Moll Flanders* and *Robinson Crusoe,* or Richardson trying to write *Pamela* and *Clarissa,* in Latin.

Latin, like Hebrew, was in continuous literary use through the late Renaissance for discursive writing and poetry (one recalls that both Milton and Donne wrote Latin verse). But it was, of course, irrelevant to the new serious representation of contemporary everyday reality which culminated the vernacular revolution in European literatures. Hebrew, on the other hand, was not a lingua franca of the erudite but had powerful associations with the concrete historical experience of the Jewish people; it was at once a learned language, the possession of an educated elite, and symbolically—though not actually—a popular one. Consequently, nineteenth-century writers striving to create a new Jewish culture integral to European modernity conceived the paradoxical project of representing quotidian reality in a language nobody spoke but which, under the aspect of eternity that has always been the measure of Hebrew literature, everyone ought to have spoken.

In this seemingly quixotic undertaking, the distinctive historical linguistics of Hebrew constituted both a problem and, in the course of time, the beginnings of a solution. Hebrew has been in continuous literary use for about three thousand years. Because of the powerful authority of the Bible for all subsequent Hebrew writers, both religious and secular, the earliest stages of the language have remained intelligible to, and adaptable by, modern readers—there are not two languages, like modern and classical Greek. Rather, there is a development within the same language, encompassing changes perhaps no greater than from sixteenth-century English to contemporary English. To be sure, three thousand years and contacts with many different languages (Akkadian, Aramaic, Greek, Latin, Persian, Arabic, and so forth) have produced half a dozen or more historical strata in Hebrew, but for the purposes of literary style, it will suffice to keep in mind the two major historical layers: biblical and rabbinic Hebrew.[3] The two differ significantly—despite manifold continuities—in grammar, syntax, and vocabulary.

The biblical verb system has only two formal indications of tenses, usually referred to by grammarians as perfect (*pa'al*) and imperfect (*yif'al*). From where we stand, it is a little difficult to reconstruct how time was actually divided by this formal distinction. Some have argued that the forms designate not tenses but aspects of verbs—that is, indications of whether an action is complete or incomplete. Syntactic or adverbial signals sometimes give verbs a pluperfect or iterative sense. In any event, the distinction between past and future does not seem as absolute as in European languages, and the segmentation of time through the tense system is not as elaborate as in European languages. The prevailing biblical syntax is paratactic—that is, a stringing together of parallel structures, without much syntactic subordination, "and" being the most common connective term between clauses (though certain contextual clues convert this formal indicator in biblical Hebrew into a signal for "but," "also," and so forth). In terms of vocabulary, the Bible works with a relatively limited palette, perhaps because its narrative conventions involve very little descriptive specification.

All this changed in the new Hebrew of the sages that emerged in the last two centuries B.C.E. and that was put to literary use in the primary code of rabbinic law, the Mishnah, in the third century C.E., and in the Midrash, beginning in the fourth century C.E. At least in part through the pressure of the Aramaic vernacular, the Hebrew tense system now was given a clear-cut past, present, and future, together with an iterative or habitual past. Certain archaic grammatical forms were regularized and simplified. The biblical habit of parataxis was frequently set aside for the causal and relational specifications of a syntax of subordination; to that end a spate of new subordinate conjunctions was introduced into the language. The legal discourse of the Mishnah involved naming the minute details of realia, and in parallel fashion, the familiar anecdotal style of the Midrash often required an evocation of the bathhouses, the slave markets, the inns, and the imperial courts of the late-antique world. In consequence, the language of rabbinic literature was flooded with new terms specifying everyday realities, borrowed from Aramaic, Greek, and Latin.

Although rabbinic Hebrew represented an enormous lexical expansion of the language, it also often introduced new terms to *replace* older ones. This meant that a whole new order of synonymity entered the language, which would prove both a resource and a source of perplexity for later generations of writers. The situation was roughly analogous to that of English after the Norman Conquest, when the major infusion of French produced many overlapping terms that were gradually differentiated through usage. In the case of Hebrew, the pattern of differentiation, whether in regard to the stylistic level or the actual meanings of the competing terms, would long remain uncertain, without any predictable pattern. For example, both biblical *shemesh* and rabbinic *ḥamah* meant "sun," and it was by no means clear whether there might be nuances of different associations, or different stylistic levels, between the two words. H. N. Bialik, at the end of his extraordinary poem "Splendor" ("*Zohar*"), transforms the sun, *shemesh,* which in the body of the poem was a source of visionary experience, into the rabbinic *ḥamah,* a mere source of heat (the transparent etymology of *ḥamah*), but his differentiation is purely ad hoc.

The choice between biblical and rabbinic Hebrew was a crucial one for early modern Hebrew literature. Although the prose of the Haskalah was by no means consistently biblical, it evinced a pronounced biblicizing tendency. There were both negative and positive motives for this seemingly odd preference. Rabbinic Hebrew was associated in many minds with the latter-day rabbis, with the narrow learning of *shtetl* and ghetto, with all that the new literati were trying to put behind them in the creation of an enlightened modern Hebrew culture. The language of the Bible, on the other hand, had an aura of cultural prestige: sublime thoughts had been expressed in that Hebrew; it could be imag-

ined as a kind of epic precedent for later literature, breathing the
same grandeur and dignity as Homer and Virgil.

Here I must mention a peculiarity of Hebrew literary compe-
tence that may seem implausible to our own amnesiac age. Over
the centuries, most people who have written Hebrew have known
the Bible virtually by heart and have counted on a similar knowledge in their readers. The great medieval poets like Judah Halevi
and Solomon ibn Gabirol make their texts an unbroken weave of
intricate biblical allusions, very often producing extraordinary
resonances by playing their own experience against the recollection of the biblical passages from which they draw their language.
But the Haskalah writers, with a self-consciousness in their relation to biblical antecedents of which their literary predecessors
had been free, transformed this tradition of allusion into what I
would call a cult of the biblical phrase. *Melitsah* is a term that
means poetry (or perhaps one should say "poesy"), rhetoric, and,
in the eighteenth and nineteenth centuries, the high-flown biblical phrase. Biblical poetry in particular was mined for such
phrases: merely to invoke a figure of speech, a rhetorical maneuver, a *recherché* term from Isaiah, Job, Psalms, or Song of Songs
was felt to imprint a magic, to confer a special status on an idea or
object. Thus, a Haskalah writer would not simply say that something soared or bounded but that it was "like the sparks that fly
upward" (Job 5:7); a landscape would be not merely pleasing to
the eye but "beautiful of situation, the joy of the whole earth"
(Psalms 48:2); Odessa would be not just a mercantile city but
"merchant of the people for many isles" (Ezekiel 27:3); even a
simple verb like "to kiss" would characteristically be elaborated
into "let him kiss with the kisses of his mouth" (Song of Songs
1:2) because of the momentum of the lofty scriptural precedent.
The biblical phrase served a function in Haskalah writing analogous to the introduction of iconology and mythology in the novels of Balzac. Just as Balzac self-consciously sought to elevate his
whores, misers, and social climbers into the protagonists of im-
mortal art by representing them as Madonnas, Jesus Christs, and

Adonises, even so the *melitsah,* lifted from its classical Hebrew contexts and slapped down on contemporary realities, was meant by its mere application to give the dignity of the ages to contemporary objects of representation.[4]

It is hardly surprising that the style frequently engendered by this cult of the phrase should be a lifeless pastiche of biblical fragments. The first Hebrew novel, Avraham Mapu's *The Love of Zion* (*'Ahavat Tsiyon,* 1853), was set in the age of Isaiah and so offered a convenient historical motivation for its rhapsodic biblical style. But when Hebrew novelists turned to the contemporary world, as Mapu himself and others did beginning in the 1860s, their biblicizing bent led them into enormous difficulties. Because nobody actually spoke Hebrew at the time, the contradictions are most spectacular in dialogue, as, for example, when a husband tries to calm his shrewish wife, irritated by the household help, in these words: "Comfort thee, comfort thee, for the Lord hath given thee rest from thy sorrow and thy trouble and from the hard labor." The quotation is from the first chapter of a short novel called, with a didactic flourish, *Learn to Do Well* (*Limdu Heytev*), published in 1862 by a twenty-six-year-old writer named Shalom Yakov Abramowitz. In 1868 he would reissue it with substantial revisions and a new, Turgenevian title, *Fathers and Sons* (*Ha'avot vehabanim*), by which it has since been known. The novel, Abramowitz's first, was a teetering, ungainly thing. He himself clearly sensed this, for, after revising *Fathers and Sons,* he gave up on Hebrew for the next eighteen years, producing instead a brilliant series of satiric novels in Yiddish about Jewish life in the Pale of Settlement through the mediating persona of Mendele the Bookseller. Writing as Mendele, he became the acknowledged "grandfather" of the Yiddish novel. When he returned to Hebrew in 1886, creating new stories and reworking his Yiddish novels into Hebrew, he was in a position to become one of the prime inventors of modern Hebrew prose. In order to appreciate the difficulties he overcame, we should first have a brief look at the Hebrew Abramowitz before Mendele.

*Fathers and Sons* offers certain signs of stylistic vigor, and Abramowitz's mastery of the whole range of historical resources of the language is evident, but a constant undertow of biblical usage pulls the characters toward depths that have nothing to do with their represented experience. The absurdities, as I have noted, are most patent in dialogue, but the narrator himself often has difficulty in fighting free from the cult of the phrase. Here is a brief evocation (chapter 2, 1912 edition) of further domestic hullabaloo presided over by the ever-irate Sarah, whom we observed a moment ago as the object of her husband's words of comfort:

> After a few minutes one could hear from Shimon's room voices talking, *the voice of Efraim and the voice of Shimon.* And in the cookhouse *a voice from the heights was heard, Sarah rebuking the people of her house,* and servants *rushing off, hastened and pressed,* and the cry of roosters and fattened geese rose to the heavens.

The phrases I have emphasized are all drawn from familiar classical Hebrew sources; it is immediately apparent that about half the words in the passage are assemblages of such prefabricated units, a fairly typical proportion for Haskalah prose. There is only one nonbiblical allusion: "rushing off" (*yehafezun*). Though only a single word in the Hebrew, this would have been recognized by readers because of its unusual grammatical form as a term from the solemn *unetaneh toqef* prayer from the High Holiday liturgy, in which angels rush off as the dread Day of Judgment approaches. Let me spell out the biblical allusions. A simple indication of two men talking, "the voice of Efraim and the voice of Shimon," echoes a repeated refrain in Jeremiah (e.g., 7:34), "the voice of gladness and the voice of joy." The link is reinforced by an intertextual rhyme, *Shimon* and *sason* ("gladness"). Whether or not the cookhouse (or perhaps kitchen, such terms being often uncertain in nineteenth-century Hebrew) is supposed to sit on a second story, or whether the lady is standing on a bench, "a voice from the heights was heard, Sarah rebuking the people of her house," so that the narrator can introduce a joking citation of Jeremiah 31:15: "a voice from the heights was heard, lamentation and bitter weeping; Rachel weeping for her children," with the last phrase being a reversal rather than a citation of the biblical source, "rebuking" substituted for "weeping." Even the scurrying about of the servants, "hastened and pressed," invokes a biblical formula, the urgent haste of Ahasuerus's messengers in Esther 8:14.

It would have been easy to choose a text from *Fathers and Sons* in which the biblical allusions were mere dead weight, in which the young Abramowitz was simply in thrall to the magic of the *melitsah* (as was generally true of the earliest version). Our example is more instructive about the style of the later Abramowitz precisely because of the ambiguous function of its allusions. In the original version of 1862, the passage is a pastiche of inert citations, mostly biblical. When Abramowitz subjected the novel to a final revision in the 1912 edition of his collected works, from which I have quoted, he tried to introduce changes in keeping with his later stylistic practice, but he was not altogether successful. Clearly, some attempt has been made to generate a comic dissonance between the classical phrases and the modern scene they are made to describe: instead of a compassionate mother Rachel, a scolding matron Sarah; instead of rushing angels (an allusion already present in the 1862 version) or messengers, domestic servants. But the invocation of "the voice of gladness and the voice of joy" seems gratuitous; the allusion to weeping Rachel has a somewhat ambiguous ironic justification, and the allusion to the Persian imperial messengers remains unfocused, leaving a margin of doubt as to whether a real satiric point is being made or whether the prose is simply trapped in a kind of Hebrew echo chamber.

The predominant language of *Fathers and Sons* is biblical, in accordance with Haskalah practice, though insets of varying length employ rabbinic language. When Abramowitz revised the novel in his old age, he made these insets much more abundant. What is historically significant in regard to the adaptability of the strata of Hebrew to new literary uses is that this text, which remains awkward even after two revisions, exhibits the beginnings of a division of labor between the two Hebrews. Let me offer one example where such a division is used to give a special Hebrew definition to a familiar narrative convention of the nineteenth-century European novel. Instructively, the earlier versions lack the rabbinic component and are a good deal more biblically florid. The shift from biblical to rabbinic is far more evident in the Hebrew than in translation because it involves not only diction but grammar, as the narrator moves from the biblical tense system (perfect and imperfect verbs) to the rabbinic (in this case, the historical present, that is, present for past, a device used in several European literatures but also adumbrated in the Midrash). I have italicized not just biblical citations but all conspicuously biblical locutions. The passage begins chapter 4 of the 1912 edition of the novel:

> *The doors of the gates of the east were opened, the dawn came forth in purple raiment* in honor of the approaching day of Hoshana-Rabba, *and from the brightness before it, the borders of the heavens* reddened *and all the houses of the city were revealed, and the capitals of the houses of prayer, builded as for an armory, turned gold—and Hebrews moved through the streets.* Some go down to bathe in a place of water, others come up from there with dripping earlocks, some wearing holiday garb go to the house of God, carrying palm branches and citrons.

The novelistic convention Abramowitz adopts here is to begin a scene with a panoramic overview, including nature, then to move in the focus to a crowd of people within the large scene, and then to settle on a particular figure or set of figures—the sentence following our excerpt begins: "A certain woman. . . ." (An exemplary instance of the convention is the opening passage of Dickens's *Little Dorrit,* which moves from a panorama of the port of Marseilles, to a view of the houses, to the prison, and then to one prison cell.) Interestingly, Abramowitz makes this narrowing of focus correspond to a shift in historical strata of Hebrew. Biblical language is associated by Haskalah precedent with nature and the sublime, so the first stage of description here is heavily biblicized, with the intention of giving the scene a grandeur that is both epic and lyric. There are a couple of explicit citations—"from the brightness before it [or him]" is a phrase from David's victory psalm (Psalm 18:12), and "builded as for an armory" is an often-invoked rhetorical flourish of obscure meaning from the Song of Songs 4:4. The image of the dawn coming forth in bright raiment alludes more obliquely to the simile of the dawn as bridegroom in Psalm 19:5. Otherwise, the biblical character of the language is a matter of poetic diction, and some of this is evident only in the Hebrew (the word for "city," for example, is not the usual ʿir but the loftier qiryah). The epic distancing through style continues as far as the first mention of people: the inhabitants of this small town in the Pale of Settlement are not Jews but "Hebrews"; they do not bustle or crowd through the streets but, more decorously and more vaguely, "move" (venaʿu). Then the grammar, syntax, and vocabulary all shift to the more intimate forms of rabbinic Hebrew as we watch these earlocked Jews, armed with the appurtenances of the holiday ritual, heading to synagogue.

Abramowitz does not maintain this separation of styles with perfect consistency. In a thoroughly rabbinic sentence, he cannot resist a biblical and hence "epic" reference to the place of worship as a "house of God" rather than a "synagogue." And in the next sentence, after a particular woman is introduced in the historical present, when she reaches the doorway of the synagogue "the wellsprings of her tears burst open, and she shed them before Him who dwells in the heavens." The biblicizing is apparent not only in the use of poetic cliché and epithet ("wellsprings of her tears," "Him who dwells in the heavens") but also in the fact that the entire clause falls into the symmetrical cadence and neat division of biblical poetic parallelism. As with the biblical resonances at the very beginning of the passage, the invocation of Scripture is dictated by a concern for dignity—in this case, not the dignity of the sublime but the dignity of pathos. Elsewhere, biblical language is also flourished, with echoes of Proverbs and Ecclesiastes, when the narrator strives for didactic generalization, which he conceives to be philosophic statement. In all these instances, Abramowitz falls prey to the Haskalah illusion that the subject could be elevated by the mere act of bedecking it with language from the corpus of texts that had been redefined by the new aestheticizing Hebrew writers as the model of high culture. In his later phase, he would altogether abandon the pursuit of the sublime, concluding that the Bible had to be inserted in contemporary reality in a radically different way, though even the later Abramowitz would never entirely free himself of the false allure of pathos.

During the two decades after the publication of *Fathers and Sons,* Abramowitz, who now signed his books with the name of his persona, Mendele, worked steadily at unlocking the literary resources of the eastern European Jewish vernacular, Yiddish. When he returned to writing Hebrew in 1886 with the story "Hidden Thunder" (*"Beseter ra'am"*), he was no longer content to use the language as a stiff brocade of ornamental phrases from the classical sources. Although Hebrew was still strictly a literary language—its revival as a spoken language would not build momentum until the second and third decades of our own century, and then chiefly in Palestine—Mendele now sought, against all historical logic, to make Hebrew sound as though it were the living language of the Jews about whom he wrote. He worked to give it the suppleness, the colloquial vigor, and the nuanced referential precision of the Yiddish he had fashioned during his years of growth to artistic maturity. Amazingly, he succeeded in effecting this transformation of style beyond all reasonable expectation. Suddenly, in both the language of the narrator and in the dialogue, characters seemed not paste-ups of phrases from the sources but figures that might really have lived in the nineteenth-century *shtetl,* vigorous inhabitants of an "as if" Hebrew world. On the simple level of description and narrative report, it was suddenly possible to evoke with the most vivid persuasiveness two Jews sweating in a bathhouse, or a man patiently filling his pipe, lighting it with a glowing coal held in tongs, puffing it up, and

relaxing into the pleasure of a leisurely smoke. How did Mendele
bring all this about?

His most decisive move was to set rabbinic rather than biblical
Hebrew as the normative framework of his prose. This shift made
possible a greater precision in the system of verb tenses; a more
flexible and varied syntax that allowed more nuanced specification
of relations among statements; and a wealth of vocabulary—even
excluding new coinages, in which he had some share—for naming
the minute acts, the physical appurtenances, the colors and textures and smells of ordinary experience. There was also a certain
tonal fit between the Jews of the Pale who inhabited Mendele's
stories and novels and the Hebrew in which they were represented, for at least the males among them were, after all, study-
house Jews who since childhood had been conning Rashi's commentary on the Torah, the Mishnah, early and late compilations
of midrashic lore, and perhaps devotional tracts or collections of
Hasidic teachings and tales. I do not mean to romanticize or
exaggerate the learning, which would often have been spotty or
skewed, but rather to suggest that the very ne'er-do-well wool-
gathering of these Jews was done through the idiom of these
texts, so that the rabbinic Hebrew in which Mendele represents
them is flesh of their flesh, bone of their spiritual bone, though
their real-life counterparts would in fact have been speaking and
dreaming and counting in Yiddish. Mendele's new prose, moreover, is historically comprehensive. It abounds in biblical elements, used in special ways to which we will presently attend,
but these are now the insets, not the framework. The governing
idiom, syntax, grammar, and word morphology are all rabbinic,
but other and later layers of the language are represented at points
where a nuance is needed or a particular allusion seems appropriate. These would include the liturgy, medieval philosophic prose,
the medieval and Renaissance exegesis, rabbinical responsa, poetry and prose from the Spanish belletristic tradition, devotional
literature, and at least some of the lexical innovations of Haskalah
writing.

Haim Nahman Bialik, the major figure of modern Hebrew poetry—who saw himself as Mendele's disciple and actually translated one of Mendele's novels, *The Book of Beggars* (*Sefer haqabtsanim;* in Yiddish, *Fishke the Lame*), into a Hebrew scarcely distinguishable from the master's—summed up this whole stylistic achievement in a brief essay in 1910 by proclaiming Mendele "the creator of the *nusakh.*" A *nusakh* (*nosakh* in the proper Hebrew pronunciation that Bialik, as a Yiddish-speaker, would not have used) is a traditional musical mode for chanting prayers in public worship. Anyone with a musical ear can learn a *nusakh;* once you know it, you can intone any set of words from the service and so act as prayer-leader. Its three most prominent features are its transmissibility (Bialik stresses that the *nusakh* is a collective possession), its adaptability to new circumstances (any text can be sung to it), and its status as clarified, defined form. The *nusakh* as Bialik speaks of it, suggestively rather than analytically, also bears a strong relation to what a Romantic ideologue would have called the national genius. Mendele is said to have refined, "drop by drop," whatever he found "in the treasure-house of the people's creative spirit." His personal achievement as stylist thus assumed a kind of anonymity. Still another image Bialik uses to elucidate his original metaphor of cantorial *nusakh* is "solid coinage," and what this points to is a consistency and unity among the various elements of style that imbue it with a quality of classical wholeness and stability. As Bialik recognized clearly more than seventy-five years ago, Mendele's new prose quickly became the common means of expression of a whole school of writers. The appeal of the *nusakh* was so powerful that it required (as we shall see) a willed effort of a new generation of writers to resist it. Though Hebrew today, more than six decades after its revival as a healthy vernacular, usually marches to a different drummer, one still sometimes encounters surprising bits and pieces of *nusakh* writing in contemporary Hebrew fiction and even in Israeli journalism.

The creation of the *nusakh* was in fact an extraordinary achievement, but it also entailed certain limitations upon what could be done in realistic fiction; so if writers had gone no further than the model of Mendele, the invention of Hebrew prose would not have been complete. An extended example will give a more concrete sense of this achievement. It will also afford an opportunity for reflection on the intrinsic limitations of the new style. I have chosen a passage from a story originally written in Hebrew, which will obviate consideration of the intricate issue of self-translation, though it should be noted that the challenge of translating his own prose from Yiddish to Hebrew was a major stimulus for Abramowitz's refashioning of the classical language.[5] The story, written in 1890, is called "Shem and Japheth on the Train" ("*Shem vaYefet ba'agalah*").

Literally, the title reads "on the Wagon," for Mendele the narrator, accustomed to making his circuit in the Pale of Settlement with a broken-down horse and rickety wagon, is in great bewilderment undertaking his first railroad trip and scarcely has the right term for the vehicle. (The ambiguity is encouraged by an interference from Yiddish, in which *vagon* means both "traincar" and "wagon.") Mendele himself, we should keep in mind, is a Jew in kaftan and earlocks; the books he peddles are not, God forbid, novels and poems but prayerbooks, pious pamphlets, and religious calendars. The third-class carriage is overflowing with a bustling crowd of ragtag passengers, most of them Jews, many of them refugees displaced from Prussia by a Bismarckian decree banishing resident aliens. Here, in the first chapter of the story, is Mendele's initial description of the family in whose company he finds himself:

> An *ill-favored* woman with a *lean* nose was sitting opposite me on a large pillow, from which feathers were sticking out and flying off into the air. Her eyes were timid, the skin of her lips dry and cracked, her face shriveled like a baked apple. Since her arrival she had not had a moment's rest from her children, who were pestering her with their requests and bickerings. Three of them, the smallest of the lot, were busy changing places next to their mother, popping up and down and poking her from both sides. In her lap a baby was drowsing after having wailed till its *throat was hoarse; a tear still stood on its cheek,* which was bloodless as a mustard-seed, and the infant breathed heavily. And beside me sat

her husband, a Jew in all his features: a tall and spare man, his neck lean and his back a bit bent, his nose long and his beard barely grown. There was hidden sorrow in his eyes, and on his lips the hint of a bitter smile.

English readers may detect in the energy of the writing, in the touches of caricature, in the note of pathos of the weeping babe, features reminiscent of Dickens, whom Mendele had read in Russian or Yiddish translation. Gogol would have been another model for such satiric description tinctured with compassion. The very possibility of emulating this nineteenth-century tradition of comic-grotesque prose was predicated on Mendele's embracing rabbinic Hebrew with its capacity for supple syntactic subordination. In the passage we are considering, the sentences are relatively short; elsewhere, more typically, sentences are long and serpentine, laying out chains of descriptive details through elaborate loops of clause after clause. Quite like Dickens and Gogol is the salient use of simile—"shriveled like a baked apple," "bloodless as a mustard-seed"—which Mendele characteristically draws from the homiest domestic details and from the most undignified corners of the animal realm: dried prunes, broken plates, and blackened pots; rats, lizards, and vermin. What needs some explanation is how this comic-grotesque prose is cast in the mold of a distinctive Hebrew *nusakh*.

Allusion still plays an important role, but it is more sparingly used and more carefully focused thematically, with no suspicion that the writer has simply been caught up in the momentum of the classical phrases. There are only two pairs of brief biblical allusions—again I have italicized them—in the passage (a mere nine words in the Hebrew), but they are both quite telling, in different ways. The woman, to render her epithets more literally than I have done in the excerpt, is "ill-favored and lean-nosed," like the cows in Pharaoh's dream, who are "ill-favored and lean-fleshed" (Genesis 41:3). The play on the scriptural verse is a shrewd joke with a large thematic implication. Instead of the expected "flesh" (*basar*), we get "nose" (*ḥotem*), which serves

Mendele's general propensity to imagine the nose as a synecdoche for the whole person—combining, as it were, an observation of Jewish physiognomy with a reading of the famous Gogol
story. Satirically, the allusion invites us to see the poor woman
as an emaciated cow (in this case, the grotesque animal simile is
hidden beneath the surface), while the general recollection of
Pharaoh's dream also involves the seven wasting years of famine,
which, in turn, lead to the displacement of Israel from their
land and to their enslavement in Egypt—all of this being grimly
appropriate to the plight of the woman and her family and
scores of thousands of Jews like them in the year 1890. Every-
where in the *nusakh* style, allusion measures the gap between the
God-governed grandeur of the biblical era and the shambling
reality of eastern European Jewry. Sometimes, as here, the allusion marks both a discrepancy and a similarity between the two
historical orders; elsewhere, it serves merely to expose ironic
discrepancy.

Mendele's resourcefulness in using allusion in this way is
unlimited. The story begins with phrases that recall the shout-
ing of the Israelites in the episode of the Golden Calf (Exodus
32:18), for as always with Mendele's Jews, profit taking is at
issue. Then we see the Jews forcing their way onto the crowded
train "with a strong hand and outstretched arm," as God took
Israel out of Egypt in the ancient exodus (Deuteronomy 4:34);
and at the end of the first paragraph of the story, Mendele finds
himself shoved next to a woman, with "the heaps upon heaps of
her belongings and blankets for me a wall on my right and on
my left"—the language in which the parting of the Reed Sea is
described in another moment from the biblical exodus (Exodus
14:22). And so it goes from sentence to sentence and passage to
passage, the play of biblical insets sometimes being a local joke,
sometimes offering a larger frame of thematic reference, almost
always pointing comically to a gap between the biblical source
and the modern object of representation.

The second pair of allusions in our excerpt is not comic; it underlines a consonance rather than a dissonance between biblical and modern. Allusions of this sort are far less frequent than the satiric sort and are generally reserved for moments, like this one, when Mendele wants an effect of pathos. The baby has a tear on its cheek (*dim'ato* . . . *'al lehyo*), like widowed Zion at the beginning of Lamentations (1:2). Its throat is hoarse from crying, like that of the suppliant in Psalm 69:4: "I am weary of my crying: my throat is hoarse: mine eyes fail while I wait for my God." Here, then, the allusion serves to align the infant refugee with a timeless picture of Jewish suffering, and the recollection of the whole verse from Psalms helps to spell out the larger theological sense of desperation that such calamity requires. Pathos of this sort may no longer be to our taste, and allusion in Mendele is for the most part used more ironically, but it is worth noting that even in consonant, nonsatiric allusion, Mendele exerts a fine control over the appropriateness of the biblical texts to the modern situations he represents.

Allusion is an ingredient of the new style, but the creation of the *nusakh* depends on more pervasive features of language. Mendele and his stylistic followers for the next two generations, down to Haim Hazaz, who died in 1973, are celebrated for the sense of realistic fullness they evoke in their writing. Realistic fullness is, of course, an illusion in which we enter willingly as readers, because any literary account of a scene, an event, or a human figure is necessarily a drastic selection of all the observable details. How is this illusion produced in *nusakh* writing? To begin with, abundant use is made of catalogues, a device native to the nineteenth-century novel rather than to Mendele's rabbinic sources. This device operates incipiently in our passage in the brief chains of descriptive details, and more elaborately elsewhere in the story. When you send your dirty linen to the laundry, you put everything on the laundry list, so the very form of the list as it is adopted by novelists conveys the assumption of completeness. That assumption is reinforced by the high degree of synonymity cultivated in the *nusakh* style, which is evident in our passage:

when so many overlapping attributes are stated, one assumes that everything that needs to be said has been said. The overlapping terms, moreover, are characteristically arranged in balanced pairs and triplets, which gives the prose an effect of solidity, symmetry, finality—the "solid coinage" of style to which Bialik referred. Thus, the woman is "ill-favored and lean-nosed"; her physiognomy is rendered as a triadic series—eyes, lips, and face. Within this series, the epithets ascend by stages from a single term, "timid," to a pair, "dry and cracked," to a metaphorical elaboration, "shriveled like a baked apple." Again, the husband is symmetrically rendered in a series of three paired items: "tall and spare," "neck . . . and . . . back," "nose . . . and . . . beard." The symmetry of the final sentence—"There was hidden sorrow in his eyes, and on his lips the hint of a bitter smile"—is somewhat different, vaguely recalling the parallel clauses of biblical poetry, but it fits perfectly with the powerful sense of balance that is one of the hallmarks of the *nusakh*.[6]

Let me recapitulate the principle features of this prose. Fullness is achieved through cataloguing and synonymity; and liveliness, through the salient grotesque metaphors and the rich play of comic allusion. A sense of definitiveness is achieved through the repeated deployment of balanced structures; and unity, through the general adherence to the grammatical and syntactical norms of rabbinic Hebrew. To this one must add a characteristic that, like the last one, is more evident in the original Hebrew than in translation: there is a constant flaunting of the linguistic medium as it is being used to represent the contemporary world. The pleasure of such texts derives from a tacit compact between writer and reader that they share an abundant culture of classical language which the writer will continuously exhibit with the most inventive virtuosity, counting on the knowing reader for repeated recognition of the skill of verbal prestidigitation. A crucial aspect of style—in which both this flaunting of language and the effect of unity are palpable—is the use of idiom. Beyond any consideration of allusion (including allusions to specific rabbinic texts), the *nusakh* style assumes that if there are indigenous Hebrew ways to say things, that is, how a good writer must say them. Our passage offers one modest instance—the feathers that "were sticking out and flying off into the air." The last phrase, in Hebrew, is *'avir ha'olam* (literally, "the world's air"). This turn of speech has no equivalent in modern European languages, but it is the idiomatic way in rabbinic Hebrew of referring to "the light of day" into which a living creature is born, or to empty space, especially when things go flying into or sailing through it.

Every language, of course, has its own stockpile of distinctive idioms, but among the modern Western languages there is also a body of shared idioms, abundantly used by writers. That is one reason for the relative ease of mutual translatability of, say, English and French prose. To conceive the texture of *nusakh* writing, one might imagine as an English equivalent a flamboyantly down-home American stylist who would brandish in every sentence expressions like "you could have knocked me for a loop," "sharp as a tack," "clean as a hound's tooth." There are, for example, several ways, both nonfigurative and figurative, current in European languages for indicating a switch or confusion of proper order: "getting signals crossed," "doing something topsy-turvy" (or, more pungently, "ass-backwards"), or "putting the cart before the horse." Israeli Hebrew, with its great porosity to English, French, German, and, before these, Russian, constantly absorbs such idioms; but the *nusakh* writers take pains to say things in a native Hebrew way. Thus, a confusion of order would be, in proper rabbinic idiom, *lahafokh 'et haq'arah 'al piha* ("to turn the bowl upside down"), or, in a postrabbinic phrase, *lehahalif 'et hayotsrot* ("to switch the *yotsrot*"). A *yotser* (the singular form) is a liturgical poem inserted in the morning service just before the blessing for the daily renewal of light. Someone who switched the *yotsrot* would be a prayer-leader who began to recite the *yotser* for Passover on Sukkot, or vice versa. The example is symptomatic, for the idiom is not one that could have arisen in London or Vienna or Moscow because it reflects the distinctive

historical experience of the Jewish people, in this case involving
the ritual conventions that were part of the familiar fabric of
collective existence. The subjects, to be sure, of the new writing
might often be far removed from synagogue and study-house, but
the language in which such subjects were represented was steeped
in the values of Torah and prayer and commandments that had
defined Jewish life from the first centuries of the Common Era to
the modern age. It was Mendele's ability to exploit these accumulated resources of expression, and to teach others how to exploit
them, that led Bialik to celebrate his achievement as a distillation
from "the treasure-house of the people's creative spirit."

The *nusakh,* then, after the stylistic fumblings of the Haskalah,
is a grand triumph, vibrant with linguistic energy, sure in the
mastery of its own verbal register, full of lively invention and
exquisitely literate play. But, as certain young Hebrew writers in
the first decade of the twentieth century began to feel, it was also
unsuited to some of the most important tasks of modern fiction.
Increasingly, Hebrew writers were concerned with conceptual and
experiential fields that had not been shaped by the *yeshivot* and the
houses of prayer, and they were dissatisfied with a language redolent of those institutions which could be applied to the modern
world only through a constant and ingenious exercise of ironic
imagination.

There is a poignant moment in "Shem and Japheth on the
Train" that inadvertently concedes this discrepancy between language and world through its very ingenuity. Mendele is baffled
when Reb Moshe, the refugee tailor he meets on the train, tells
him there are no more Jews in the world (what Reb Moshe has in
mind is that the new German doctrine has redefined Jews racially
as Semites). When Mendele is asked whether he knows what age
he is living in, he responds indignantly:

> "I don't know! . . . Why, here's my calendar, printed at my
> own initiative and expense. Today's the fourth day of the week of
> the Torah-reading Korah, in the year five thousand six hundred
> and forty according to the full reckoning."—I counted out the

number of years and days since the creation of the world in a loud
voice all in one breath, taking out one of the little calendars I had
in my pocket, brandishing it and showing the print to Moshe, also
intending by the way to make an announcement, so that people
would know I had calendars for sale.

"But that's not how it is according to the Germans," Reb Moshe
said with quiet deliberation. "The Germans with all their research, who are great inventors, have turned back the wheel of
time a thousand generations, and now all of us are living today in
the time of the Deluge. Nowadays they call a Jew 'Shem' and a
non-Jew 'Japheth.' Again we have Shem and Japheth; and with
them, again we have the practice of that ancient generation, *and
the earth is filled with violence.*"

The exchange is a kind of dramatic elaboration of the device of
ironic allusion that is the life of Mendele's prose. (The italics, of
course, are mine.) A teasing congruence between Primeval History and contemporary events is revealed with comic brilliance:
once again, as supposedly civilized people speak about Semites
and Aryans, epidemic depravity raises the threat of global catastro-
phe. The problem is that the gap between ancient text and modern world can be bridged only by the deft reach of satiric wit. In
regard to historical forces, ideological currents, technological
changes like the railroad, Mendele is not living in the year 5640,
as he imagines, but in the alien reality of 1890. The richly
textured Hebrew that he—or rather, Abramowitz behind him—
has woven out of the varied threads of tradition can show quite
luminously where he has come from, but only by indirection
where he and his contemporaries now are.

The western novel in general exhibits a broad spectrum of
stylistic possibilities, not one normative style. To mention only
writers active in Abramowitz's lifetime, we may recall how
sharply Stendhal, Flaubert, Dickens, Melville, and Henry James
differ in diction, syntax, cadence, and tone. But with all these
manifest differences, the new tradition of the novel does evince a
kind of loose stylistic consensus, or a characteristic range of styles.
As a general rule, there is a close correlation between patterns of

language and patterns of thought, and there are certain kinds of cogitation, analysis, generalization, and moral evaluation that go on in the novel which are tied in to certain generic habits of style. To cite one small example that can stand for many more complicated ones, Flaubert's famous "Emma rediscovered in adultery all the platitudes of married life" is predicated on a formal tradition of moral aphorism, on a worldliness of perspective palpable in the narrator's tone, on the nuanced abstraction of the term *platitudes*—none of which would have been possible in the Hebrew of the *nusakh.* Serious novels are a way of knowing, and many of the conceptual instruments and tonal modulations of this cognitive enterprise are beyond the scope of Mendele's Hebrew.

Even more crucially, the European novel in the last decades of the nineteenth century was moving toward an experiential realism, shifting the center of narration from narratorial overviews to the minute pulsations of thought and feeling of the main characters. This movement was particularly impressive in Russia, manifested in different ways by Tolstoi and Dostoevski, then by Chekhov and, in the new century, by Andrey Bely. Mendele on his part remained faithful to Gogol, a Russian master of the previous generation; or, to put the case in English terms, he succeeded in fashioning a brilliant Hebrew equivalent of early Dickensian prose at a moment when the late Henry James was emerging—a writer he did not know and whose style of finespun ramification and qualification he could not have assimilated. What the language of the *nusakh,* for all its glories, could not do was to provide persuasive access to the consciousness of the characters, to serve the purposes of a realism that was experiential rather than social and collective. It was not only literary history or the *Zeitgeist* that impelled writers to this new project but also the inner logic of the paradoxical representation of an "as if" Hebrew world. If Yiddish-speaking and Russian-speaking Jews were to be rendered in Hebrew, then they had to have not only a social language but also an inner life that was richly, plausibly Hebrew. This was the second momentous stage of the invention of Hebrew prose that was undertaken by several gifted young writers after the turn of the century. Like the creation imagined in Lurianic Kabbalah, it could be accomplished only through a violent breaking of vessels.

# 2

# Toward
# a Language
# of
# Experience

$B$y the turn of the twentieth century, Hebrew literature in eastern Europe was an extraordinary success story—not in scale, for it remained, perforce, the movement of a tiny elite, but in quality. Its greatest center was in Odessa, where the remarkable journal *HaShiloah* was published, where Mendele reigned, and where the young poets H. N. Bialik, Saul Tchernichovsky, Yakov Steinberg, and Zalman Schneour were active; but there were also other centers, and other journals, in Vilna, Warsaw, Lemberg, and even small western outposts in London and Berlin. Some of the most innovative of the new writers of fiction who began their careers around this time felt stymied by the very solidity and the formal harmony of the *nusakh* that Mendele had established as the model of Hebrew prose. Aspiring to Chekhovian subtleties or Dostoevskian intensities, or embarked on a Nietzschean project of radically redefining received values, and in any case concentrating on the isolated, disaffected intellectual instead of the Jewish community and the typical Jew, these new Hebrew writers needed a language that could accommodate nuance, dissonance, disorder, ambiguity, and wavering inwardness as the classicizing balance and fullness of the *nusakh* could not. The achievement of Mendele was such an authoritative model of good literary Hebrew that certain of the new writers were impelled deliberately to write "bad" Hebrew in order to make the language serve new purposes. It is only a partial exaggeration to say that their implicit aim was to transform Hebrew from within into a European language.

This act of linguistic subversion was something that Bialik, always the faithful stylistic disciple of Mendele, clearly detected. In 1923, two decades after the second revolution in Hebrew prose, he advises the young Hebrew novelist Yohanan Twersky: "Gnessin and his crowd sinned in this regard to a certain extent. . . . One doesn't draw analogies from one language to another ['*eyn lemedin milashon lelashon,* itself a Talmudic, "un-European" formulation], and certainly not from an Aryan to a Semitic language."[1] Bialik's motives, let me suggest, are both nationalistic and aesthetic. In his view, a writer ought to follow the indigenous patterns of classical Hebrew because they reflect the national genius, the accumulated historical experience, of the people, and also because, by adhering to them, the literary work is endowed with stylistic consistency and formal coherence. On the other side of the barricades, the writers who rejected the *nusakh* did so in part on ideological grounds because they were proposing a new order of national experience for the Jewish people, and in part— the larger part, I think—on artistic grounds because they placed mimetic fidelity above aesthetic completeness.

An interesting case in point is Micha Yosef Berdichevsky (1865–1921), a Russian-born writer who migrated to the West to get a Ph.D. in philosophy and ended up spending most of his career in Berlin. He published his first stories in the 1890s, and they made a strong impression on younger writers like Yosef Haim Brenner (1881–1921) and Uri Nissan Gnessin (1879– 1913), who began their literary careers a decade later. To an ear attuned to the idiomatic modulations of the classic Hebrew sources, Berdichevsky's prose can often be rather grating. Though it is quite possible that he did not have as sure a feeling for the language as did some of his literary contemporaries, I suspect that to a large extent his aim was precisely to grate on traditionally formed stylistic sensibilities.

Typically in Berdichevsky's stories and novellas, the two historical strata of Hebrew—biblical and rabbinic—are promiscuously intermingled. Mendele's imposition of a rabbinic norm is rejected, perhaps because it is felt to be somehow restrictive, or more likely, because it implies on the level of style a harmony of wrought artifice that runs counter to Berdichevsky's intention to represent conditions of alienation or ambivalence and eruptions of violent desire. In his use of figurative language, though Berdichevsky does not hesitate to draw on the Bible and on rabbinic literature, he exhibits a receptivity, new in Hebrew writing, to conventional—indeed, cliché—metaphors of European literature: collocations like "depths of thought," "heights of imagination," and self-consciously symbolic statements like "until the curtain would be raised on life's enigma." I am not suggesting that it takes courage or artistic boldness to succumb to a cliché, only that this willingness to import clichés from the literary environment reflects the aspiration to make the language of the prophets and the sages sound in some ways like Standard Modern European. Especially instructive as symptoms of this undertaking are Berdichevsky's frequent errors in Hebrew idiom. Most of these cannot be shown in translation precisely because they require knowledge of the original idioms, but I can offer a few small examples where the error is visible because it involves an element of redundancy. A single story, "The Two Camps" (*"Maḥanayim"*), written toward the end of the 1890s, is sprinkled with usages such as the following: "when her lover was impoverished *from his possessions"; according to the words of people"; "his soul then longs after intimacy and privacy." In each case, Berdichevsky's familiarity with a way of putting things in another language sets up an unconscious interference with the Hebrew idiomatic pattern. The superfluous "from his possessions" after "impoverished" appears because the writer has half in mind another Hebrew idiom for impoverishment, *yarad minekhasav* (literally, "went down from his possessions"). On this he has imposed a European pattern in which a passive or reflexive verb—in the Hebrew here, *nit-daldel*—is used to indicate being impoverished. "According to *the words of* people" (*lefi divrei habriyot*) reflects the impingement of languages that invoke "what people say" (e.g., German, *was man sagt;* Yiddish, *vos mentshen zogen*), whereas the rabbinic idiom is content to use either "according to people" (*lefi habriyot*) or "by people's words" (*ledivrei habriyot*), but never both together. Finally, the verb "to long" requires a preposition that means "for" (*'el,* or sometimes *'al*), but it appears that the writer has too much in mind the German *sich sehnen nach.*

Such misusages contribute no more than a series of minor off notes to the general artistic effect of the story, but they are interesting as inadvertent reflections of Berdichevsky's predisposition to make Hebrew work as though it were a dialectal variation of standard literary European. Elsewhere, one can see the palpable gains in expression of pursuing that aim. Here are two brief sentences from chapter 3 of the same story, "The Two Camps," which I will render in the syntactic order exhibited by the Hebrew:

> Only charity they want from him, both his opponents and his teachers, and he gives all of them his contribution with a smiling face. To pray he doesn't go at all, the whole time he has been in his hometown; and to everyone it is clear that that's how it has to be.

Classical Hebrew has a good deal more flexibility in regard to the order of subject and predicate than does modern English, so the syntactic inversion at the beginning of the first sentence does not seem especially obtrusive in the original. In any case, both sentences swerve sharply from the model of Mendele in the way that syntax is used to follow the movements of thought. "Only charity they want," and then, as an explanatory afterthought appended to "they"—"both his opponents and his teachers." In the second sentence, the main object of thought, that which weighs on the awareness of the character, is placed, against the requirements of a more formal stylistic decorum, in initial syntactic position: "To pray he doesn't go at all." My guess is that here the other language Berdichevsky has in mind is not German but Yiddish (*davenen geyt er nisht*), which would also explain the unadorned, plainspoken diction of the passage.

What we have here, in sum, is a narrative technique only marginally feasible in the allusive, formally balanced language of the *nusakh:* narrated monologue, the mode of presentation in which the narrator, while continuing to mediate the experience of the character and to render it in the third person, mimes the diction, the word order, and the imagery the character would use in its unspoken inner speech. As modest as this example may

be—and one could cite more elaborate and impressive instances in
Berdichevsky—it represents a turning point in Hebrew narrative
prose. Language here is not a completed artifact, manifesting the
authorial artificer's mastery. Rather it is a means for implicating
the reader in the processes of the character's thought and feeling.
In the fiction of U. N. Gnessin, the representation of those
processes would achieve the most formidable subtlety, but before
we turn to Gnessin, I want to indicate through a different kind of
example that the primacy of process in the anti-*nusakh* writers is
observable even when what is at issue is the narrator's transactions
with the characters rather than what goes on within the characters. Here is the first paragraph of chapter 11 in Y. H. Brenner's
early novel, *Around the Point (Misaviv lanequdah,* 1903–1904).
The paragraph is a single sentence, and a rather ugly sentence at
that, certainly by the standards of the *nusakh* and perhaps by any
standards. It may be instructive to ponder the reasons for its
ugliness:

> Yakov Avramson, who had never in his life tasted childhood,
> who from the time he was little—perhaps from the age of five—
> was accustomed to investigating things beyond ordinary ken and
> to analyzing everything with a fine instrument and when he was
> little never had either various kinds of toys or little girlfriends or
> games or any other childlike things—this Avramson as an adult
> was one of those "big kids" who by nature are shrewd and grown-
> up, excessively grown-up, but when they attain a certain point of
> height their heart turns back and becomes a child's heart.

The sentence is an elaborate instance of syntactic subordination, but it is not the controlled, finely crafted kind of subordination that is set as a norm in the prose of Mendele. Instead, the
sentence proceeds through a repeated splaying out of supplemen-
tary utterances from what one hesitates to call the main assertion. That is, the main clause is: "Yakov Avramson . . . was
one of those 'big kids.' " The grammatical subject is elaborated
through a parallel series of relative clauses: "who had never . . .
tasted childhood," "who . . . was accustomed to investigating,"

"[who] never had . . . toys," and so forth. Then the predicate is elaborated through a relative clause that contains a coordinate clause: "who by nature are shrewd and grown-up . . . , but when they attain. . . . " The prime symptom of this splayed-out syntax is the abundant use of the dash, a frequent typographical recourse in the novel when the constraints of conventional syntax are broken, ever since the time of that ultimate novelist, Laurence Sterne.

What impels Brenner to this formal disorderliness, for which there is scarcely any precedent in classical Hebrew prose? In a generically typical maneuver, the narrator is trying to take the measure of a character, an activity that involves assembling an indeterminate quantity of untidy data (the first series of subordinate clauses) and referring them to a purportedly familiar framework of generalized social, moral, or psychological knowledge (the second series of subordinate clauses). We approach the character asymptotically, involved in discovering his nature through a process that has no fixed end, that can always benefit from further information and further sidelong perceptions. Language moves in what Roland Barthes has memorably called a "metonymic skid": the time he was little, perhaps from the age of five, various kinds of toys, little girlfriends, games, childlike things. On this skidding movement the narrator imposes a secondary pattern of zigzag qualification: a big kid, shrewd and grown-up, excessively grown-up, but their heart . . . becomes a child's heart. If one can entertain the hypothesis of an international language—call it *novelistic*—with characteristic patterns of presentation of data and analysis, then Brenner is thinking novelistic (say, Dostoevski, Zola, George Eliot) while writing Hebrew—unlike the *nusakh* writers, who often think Mishnaic-Midrashic-liturgic while writing novels in Hebrew. (Only the solitary genius of Agnon, who begins his career in Palestine in 1907 as a protégé of Brenner, would find a magic formula for writing rabbinic and novelistic in splendid convergence.) This language reflects a tentative, groping, arduously exploratory relation to the objects of its representation; it is precisely what makes so many novels long, often untidy, and cognitively rewarding. In all this, what remains in the Hebrew of the model of Mendele is the use of the rabbinic norms of grammar, which make possible the extreme pliability of syntax, however different the sprawl of that syntax looks from its rabbinic antecedents. The sole divergence from rabbinic grammar is in the very last verb in the passage, *"becomes* a child's heart," *vayehi lelev-yeladim,* which is in the biblical imperfect tense. The switch to a biblical tense at the very end is a common usage in this period to produce, through a small formal heightening, an effect of closure or pausal emphasis. One might render the effect in English, were it not for the coyness of the archaism, by translating the end of the sentence as follows: "their heart turns back and, lo, becomes a child's heart." This point about the final verb is worth registering because it suggests that Brenner did make artfully conscious choices about language and was ready to enlist the biblical stratum of Hebrew from time to time; if his diction exhibits a prosaic grayness and his syntax a jumbled look, these were qualities of style he cultivated quite deliberately.

In many ways, the most remarkable talent among the new Hebrew writers at the turn of the century was U. N. Gnessin, who became friends with Brenner when both were students at the *yeshivah* in Počep (a provincial town about 130 miles to the southeast of Smolensk) headed by Gnessin's father. Gnessin followed Brenner to London, where the two worked together, amidst contention, on the Hebrew journal *HaMe'orer,* then to Palestine, where he stayed only a few months. Brenner, committed to the collective endeavor of Zionism, though deeply disaffected from most of those who claimed to be carrying it out, remained in Palestine. He was murdered by Arabs in the riots of 1921. Gnessin, similarly disaffected and committed rather to individual experience and the life of consciousness, returned to eastern Europe. He died of tuberculosis in 1913 at the age of thirty-four, leaving behind a handful of early stories and four boldly original novellas on which his fame chiefly rests. These constitute the

earliest instance of fully achieved modernist prose in Hebrew, and
in the Hebrew tradition they have exerted oblique but significant
influence on writers as various as S. Y. Agnon, Simon Halkin, S.
Yizhar, and Amalia Kahana-Carmon. The stylistic evolution, however, from Gnessin onward was by
no means a simple linear development. For a long time, many
Hebrew readers viewed him as an oddity, no more than a coterie
writer who appealed to special tastes. (Such marginalization was
even more extreme in the case of David Fogel, whose prose we
will consider in the next chapter.) Meanwhile, through the middle decades of this century, the dominant forms of Hebrew style
were either continuations of the *nusakh,* or, perhaps more commonly, uneven mixtures of *nusakh* elements with the kind of
loosely organized prose characteristic of Brenner. Since the early
1960s, Gnessin, Fogel, and a few other early modernists have
been rediscovered, and certain manifestations of recent literary
Hebrew have come to resemble them in surprising ways. A close
consideration of the early modernists' technical achievement, once
slighted by criticism, reveals a great deal about the general possibilities of modern Hebrew prose.

I will offer illustrative passages from Gnessin's novella *To the
Side (Hatsidah,* 1905). The narrative situation—one can scarcely
speak of a plot—is quintessentially Gnessinian: the protagonist,
Nahum Hagzar, has returned from a sojourn in Vilna to his
provincial town, where he lingers for a period of many months,
drifting into a circle of young women. He is erotically drawn to
one or another of them but is not bold enough to act on his desire,
just as he repeatedly projects a major critical essay he will publish
but manages to write nothing. Neurasthenic sensibility, hobbled
will, frustrated imagination, the subversion of reality by fantasy,
the blurring of distinctions between the experiencing self and the
objective world—these are the subjects (subjects familiar to us
from modernists like Proust, Bely, Musil, Faulkner, Virginia
Woolf) for the treatment of which Gnessin had to make Hebrew
prose work in a wholly new way.

The innovative nature of Gnessin's undertaking is perhaps most evident in his handling of time. *To the Side,* like his other novellas, abounds in indications of temporal transitions, beginnings and ends of seasons, subjective flashbacks and flash-forwards. Time is not a fixed framework for the action, as in earlier Hebrew fiction, but is at once experiential and elusive to the grasp of experience, constantly slipping away in a movement of restless change as consciousness seeks to apprehend it. Here is a characteristic passage, which begins with a narratorial report of seasonal transition, then moves into an elaborate, emotionally fraught flash-forward:

That midsummer was inscribed deep in the hearts of the whole group and gave them enough to fill the many long days to come. And when afterward, long gossamer threads began creeping through the air and yellow leaves falling and scattering through the park walks, Hagzar would trample the fallen leaves with wild exultation and bursting energy, and he would stand straighter, his chest widening and thrust out and his face alert. Another week, another two weeks, and the sky would turn somber, and the winds would be howling, and the days would be gloomy, and the windowpanes would be shaking, and the tin roofs would be rattling—hurrah! and the mood would be buoyant, and the mind would be free, and the heart would well up and overflow, and work would be cherished and would fill the soul and enlarge the imagination. . . . Another week, another two weeks, and the nights would be dark, and the flames of the solitary streetlamps trembling, and the rains pelting down, and the swamp deep—and in the handsome, cherished room it would be warm and light and pleasant, and the divan covered with red velvet would be soft and spacious, and the faces of the fine young women would be lovely, and their lively eyes would be filled with brightness and pleasure, and Rosa's pleasing patter would flow on seductively, and Mania's careful, mischievous arguments would interrupt him abruptly, break off in the middle, and once more burst forth, and little, pale Ida, Ida whose glance was so marvelous, whose braid was so soft and lovely, this Ida would not by any means agree to sit in his lap and lay her sweet head on his chest, until he would catch her by her warm, soft forearms, and he would surely know that it was no little girl he had caught, and he would sit her down by force. Then she would yield and grow calm as a quiet lamb, and her dear hair would be so smooth and so rich and in his power, obeying his every touch.[2]

What I called a narratorial report of seasonal transition is actually restricted to the introductory adverbial clause of the second sentence: "And when afterward, long gossamer threads began creeping through the air. . . . " The true beginning of the passage is an indication of the impression that the season makes on the minds and in the memories of the human witnesses: "That midsummer was inscribed deep in the hearts of the whole group and gave them enough to fill the many long days to come." It is as though the external world had no validity or interest in and of itself but was worthy of attention only as the occasion for subjective experience, as a provisioner of feeling and memory. In this subjectivized vision of existence, very little happens definitely at a particular point in time. Instead, there is a constant recycling in consciousness of emotion and reflection; purely inner events repeat themselves in a blur that gradually moves forward toward changes or reversals of mood.

This dynamic of repetition and change explains Gnessin's fascination with moments of transition. The verb "began" (*hithilu*), followed by participial forms (here, "began creeping . . . falling . . . scattering"), predominates throughout the story, sometimes recurring half a dozen or more times in a single, brief passage. In consonance with this reorientation toward time, the simple past tense (Hebrew, *pa'al*) is largely replaced by the past continuous or iterative tense (Hebrew, *hayah po'el*), as in our second sentence, "Hagzar would trample. . . . " This tense, as we had occasion to observe earlier, is an invention of rabbinic Hebrew, abundantly used in both legal and narrative texts, but Gnessin is the first to make it the central vehicle of novelistic narration. It is a change as momentous as that effected by Flaubert when he substituted the French *imparfait*—equally a tense for repeated or habitual actions—for the historical past (*passé simple*) that had been customary in literary narratives. Indeed, much of what Erich Auerbach observes in *Mimesis* on the implications of Flaubert's shift to the imperfect tense is directly applicable to Gnessin's adoption of the iterative: "The novel is the representation of an entire human existence which has no issue. . . . Nothing particular happens in the scene, nothing particular has happened just before it. It is a random moment from the regularly recurring hours."[3]

A particularly revealing expression of the subtle refashioning of the language to render a new sense of reality is Gnessin's quiet installation of what is virtually a new Hebrew tense to complement his use of the iterative. The temporal indicator at the beginning of the third sentence, "Another week, another two weeks," also marks a transition from the narrator's point of view to narrated monologue—*not,* as many Hebrew critics have carelessly said, "stream of consciousness"—which is to say, the inner speech of the character reported from the grammatical perspective of the narrator. As is often the case, there are no unambiguous linguistic indications that we have moved into narrated monologue; clues derived rather from the substance of the statements allow us, as we read on, to attribute these statements with growing certainty to Hagzar rather than to the narrator. That is, after the reference to darkening skies and howling autumnal winds, which momentarily seems continuous with the narrator's report of seasonal atmosphere in the previous sentence, we encounter mind, mood, and heart; and from what we already know of the protagonist, the evocation of overflowing energy and productive work is surely his wishful fantasy.

Then there is a second temporal indicator, after the three suspension points introduced by the author, "Another week, another two weeks," that takes us into a whole fantasy scene of warm shelter and erotic arousal projected forward in time from the moment of early autumn when Hagzar stands among the leaves to a night of late autumn when storms rage outside. But just as nothing happens definitely at a single point in the past, nothing happens definitely at a single point in the future, and so Gnessin casts Hagzar's imaginings in a future iterative tense (Hebrew, *yihyeh po'el*), a form only occasionally attested in rabbinic and medieval Hebrew, which uses the future instead of the past tense of the verb "to be" as an auxiliary before the participial form of the verb: "the winds would be howling . . . the windowpanes would be shaking, and the tin roofs would be rattling . . . the flames of the solitary streetlamps [would be] trembling, and the rains pelting down." Literary readers will hardly be surprised at this strong link between the humble mechanics of grammar and overarching views of reality. Gnessin, by shifting the conventional balance of Hebrew tense usage and placing a central burden on what was traditionally a marginal tense, creates a new fluid sense of time—approximately, of time as Bergsonian flux,[4] not susceptible to mathematical definition or objective description, but rather an ambiguous, kinetic entity knowable through the intuition of consciousness.

The experience of flux is reinforced by the additive syntax Gnessin characteristically uses, especially visible here in the long final sentence. The effect is quite different from the parataxis of classical Hebrew. Instead of a firmly fixed frame of relatively short parallel utterances, as in biblical prose, the sentence unravels like a big ball of yarn, one *and*-clause following another: "and the nights . . . and the flames . . . and the rains . . . and in the . . . room . . . and the divan . . . and the faces. . . . " What dictates this structure is the associative movement of the character's imagination from one object or image to the next contiguous one. There is no fixed order, no hierarchy, no definite end, either in the series or in the mental process that engenders the series. Indeed, a common denominator of much modernist writing is the rejection of traditional hierarchies, and Gnessin's prose with its run-on sentences and its additive syntax is a beautiful enactment of such a rejection.

Our passage exhibits other means for dramatizing the perspective of the character. The most notable of these is the repetition of emotionally freighted terms. This repetition differs markedly from anaphora, or rhetorical repetition, which one often encounters in *nusakh* prose. Anaphora conveys the sense of a controlling authorial presence, insisting on a particular word in order to produce a calculated effect on the reader. In Hagzar's narrated monologue, on the other hand, the reader is no more than an eavesdropper, and the repetitions, which have none of the formal symmetry of anaphora, are expressions of the character's affective life. Thus, in the last two sentences, the room at the outset is lovely (*yafeh*), cherished (*ḥaviv*), and warm (*ḥamim*), and the first object discriminated within the room is the soft (*rakh*) divan. Then the young women's faces are lovely, Ida's braid is lovely, her forearms soft and warm, her head sweet (*ḥaviv*), her hair dear (*ḥaviv*), and toward the end, this pattern of affective repetition is intensified by the emotive adverb *so* linked to the key adjectives: so marvelous, so soft and lovely, so smooth and so rich. The character in this way reveals, or perhaps exposes, himself through the language he uses in his thoughts; and the very terms of the repetition may raise questions about the credibility of Hagzar's imagined future of sexual conquest. The cozy room full of women on a cold, dark night is an alluring fantasy that mingles themes of shelter and gratification which seem ultimately associated with womblike protection or infantile pleasure—the warmth, the softness, the sweetness of it all—rather than with adult sexuality.

Be that as it may, Gnessin's prose is altogether impressive in its ability to represent reflection and fantasy with a kind of sensuous immediacy. His Hebrew, moreover, has a tonal unity that avoids the grating qualities of the prose of Berdichevsky and Brenner. The general effect is very different from *nusakh* writing, but I would propose that the achievement of the *nusakh* is a precondition for Gnessin's innovations. Mendele and his disciples taught subsequent Hebrew writers how to exploit the grammatical precision and the syntactic suppleness of rabbinic Hebrew for the purposes of novelistic narration. Gnessin, fashioning a new experiential realism in Hebrew prose, repeatedly uses these rabbinic forms even as he pushes them into shapes that would have deeply puzzled the makers of the Mishnah and the Midrash. With this language, he is able to mime mental processes with the vivacity of a vernacular, even though at the time he was writing, and for the real-life counterparts of the figures about whom he was writing, there was no Hebrew vernacular.

Gnessin's representation of the inwardness of his characters is by no means limited to the technique of narrated monologue. Let me propose for consideration a second passage from *To the Side,* in which the narrative approach to consciousness proceeds along rather different technical lines. Some attention to its details should extend our sense of how Gnessin endows Hebrew prose with a new suppleness and gives it mimetic fidelity as a vehicle for fiction. In a novella where nothing really happens, Hagzar's story is a chain of incompletions, the account of a man surrounded by fragments and tail ends of objects and projects and ideas; even the letters of the words he tries to write disintegrate before his eyes into broken squiggles and scratch marks. Toward the end, Hagzar's old friend and sexual competitor Carmel appears on the scene, exhibiting a sense of adequacy that discomfits the ever inadequate Hagzar. The last, fragmentary scene of the novella takes place in Ida's room. Ida, prostrate, has been thrown into what looks like a nervous convulsion by an encounter with Car-mel; Hagzar stands by her bedside with a glass of water in his hand. This is the last paragraph of the story:

> And Hagzar suddenly felt a terrible contraction of the heart, and a hot stream of blood flooded his face and made his eyes wince. What was he doing here? A moment passed and Carmel's confi-dent laughter cut through his heart, and his eyes saw Hannah's folded arms, and his ears heard the strong laughter of the man who had put them that way. Afterward, the advertisement of the doc-tor from Vilna glimmered in his mind and vanished again. And suddenly splendid Vilna stood before him as though it were actu-ally present, and he remembered its many talmudic academies, and the Strashun Library, and his work in the reading room, and the book *Knesset Yisrael* with the handsome picture of Peretz Smolenskin, and the nights of tremendous work in his quiet room

there, and his friends dreaming the same dreams as he; and the contraction of his heart swelled to the point of choking. And then with confused consciousness he set the glass of water down on the chair and his legs stumbled toward the door. And when he went outside and a fresh breeze flowed into him, his eyes brightened a bit, and his temples were throbbing, and his heart was pounding, and he passed the end of the street and went on outside the town and walked along lazily, and his eyes were looking with sad indifference at the long long railroad tracks that stretched out before him desolate and fainting from the heat of the day.[5]

Narrated monologue in the passage is restricted to a single terse sentence: "What was he doing here?" The rest of the passage, apart from the minimal notations of Hagzar's physical movements, is made up of what Dorrit Cohn calls *psycho-narration,* that is, the report, summary, description of the movements of thought and feeling, in the language of the narrator instead of their immediate rendering in the unspoken inner speech of the character.[6] The nineteenth-century Russian novel makes rich and abundant use of this technique. My guess is that the most pertinent model for Gnessin was Dostoevski, who was so repeatedly fascinated with the spasmodic intensities of consciousness, with the distortive effects of obsession on the objects of perception. Here is Raskolnikov in *Crime and Punishment* standing on the Voznesensky Bridge:

Leaning over the water he looked mechanically at the last pink reflections of the sunset, at the row of buildings growing dark in the thickening dusk, at one distant window, high up in some roof along the left bank, that shone for an instant with flame as the last ray of the dying sun caught it, at the darkening water of the canal. Into the water he peered attentively, until at last red circles began to revolve before his eyes, the houses spun round, the passers-by, the carriages, the embankments, all reeled and swung dizzily.[7]

There are differences in proportion between Dostoevski and Gnessin that are approximately attributable to the differences between nineteenth-century realist and early modernist. Dostoev-

ski's novel, for all its concern with psychology, accords primacy
to a set of objective narrative data, in which significant events
happen in linear concatenation: an act of murder, the circumstan-
tial concreteness of the Petersburg setting, a process of discovery,
confession, punishment, and redemption. The dizzying quality of
consciousness in this brief excerpt, as elsewhere in *Crime and
Punishment,* is realistically motivated because the character in question is in a feverish, hallucinatory state. In the modernist Gnessin, mental processes rather than actions performed in the external world have become the real subject of narration, which is now
cyclical and repetitive rather than linear in structure; and it is
consciousness as such, rather than consciousness in liminal states,
that breaks things into kaleidoscopic fragments.

Elsewhere in *To the Side,* there are subjective views of landscapes
that are still closer in technique to Raskolnikov's disturbed perception here of the buildings and the canal. But what I think Gnessin
may have above all discovered in Dostoevski is that fiction could
find a language to describe compellingly the spasms and associative
jumps of consciousness itself. The last paragraph of *To the Side*
begins with a heart contraction, and it is framed by the organs of
perception and defined by a series of uneven pulsations. When
Hagzar is confronted with the evidence of Carmel's power over Ida,
heart contracts, face is flooded, eyes wince; then in a recollection of
a scene earlier that day, heart is cut through, eyes see and ears hear
remembered sights and sounds. At the end of the passage, the eyes
are again prominent, along with further attention to what might
be called the cardiovascular manifestations of emotion—throbbing
temples and pounding heart. The paragraph thus has both fluidity
and a certain symmetry, simultaneously satisfying the demands of
mimesis and aesthetic shaping, in good modernist fashion. Equally
characteristic of modernism, both of its impressionistic and expressionistic trends, is the use of synecdoche, the body's being represented by disconnected organs.[8]

Fluidity is manifested chiefly in the associative movements of
memory. Bits of recollection glimmer and vanish, like the newspa-

per advertisement of the Vilna doctor that Hagzar had noticed earlier in the day at Hannah's house. The connection with Vilna carries him back to a more distant memory of the time he spent in that city. This memory itself is not an integrated picture but a chain of associatively linked fragments: from academies to library to reading room to a photograph in a literary miscellany of the Haskalah writer, Peretz Smolenskin, and from there to the protagonist's own dreams of literary achievement. When we return, through a second terrible contraction of the heart, to the external world, Hagzar's body, like his mind, is swept along by forces not under volitional control. His legs "stumble" or "wander" (*taʿu*) toward the door in a reflexive action of escape that will, of course, amount to nothing. His eyes brighten in the open air, but only a bit and only momentarily; then, in the downsweep of inner oscillation, they look with sad indifference at the receding perspective of railroad tracks. These tracks should logically point to a way out of the emotional prison of the town and Hagzar's round of unending frustrations there, should imply a rapid conveyance to Vilna and the great world beyond. But in fact, like everything the protagonist sees, they are only an extension, an external symbol seized upon ad hoc, of his own inner plight: no train travels on these tracks that trail off to the end of vision. Appropriately reflecting the character's predicament, they lie "desolate and fainting from the heat of the day."

The distinctive traits of Gnessin's diction, not visible in translation, deserve comment because they suggest the degree of his success in the creation, at this early moment, of a living literary Hebrew. To readers of Hebrew literature in the waning years of the twentieth century, there is surely something historically prescient about this prose. Apart from a few minor exceptions, which I will explain momentarily, the style seems not at all archaic. Indeed, it sits quite comfortably on the same bookshelf with contemporary Israeli novelists, native speakers of the language like A. B. Yehoshua, Yitzhak Ben-Ner, S. Yizhar, and Amalia Kahana-Carmon. There is only one loan word in the passage, which has long since passed out of usage—*bibliotheka* for "library," which has been displaced by the indigenous *sifriah*, coined from *sefer* ("book"). The word for "railroad tracks," (*mesilah*) is a biblical term for "road" that was adopted for this sense in the nineteenth century but has been largely displaced by *pasim* (from the word for stripes, bars, tracks). The verb I have rendered as "made wince" (*salad*) is not to my knowledge used in this sense by any other writer, and, similarly, the verb that in context appears to mean "folding" arms (*naʿots*) is an idiosyncratic usage, for the usual sense, in both rabbinic and modern Hebrew, is to thrust, stab, fix.

I mention these small examples to emphasize that until a solid community of Hebrew speakers had crystallized—with a Hebrew press, schools, and official bureaucracies—writers were faced with a mechanical problem of uncertainty about the agreed meaning of some of the words they used. Sometimes the classical sources of words left a margin of ambiguity about their semantic range; sometimes there were competing or eccentric views as to precisely what modern acceptation should be assigned to a particular classical word. The only other archaic touch I can detect in the passage is the use of the biblical imperfect tense for "and he remembered." That usage, in accord with a convention of the period I mentioned in connection with Brenner (see page 51), indicates pause, closure, or sharp transition—here, the move from recent memory (that same day at Hannah's house) to deep memory (Hagzar's earlier period in Vilna). Given the relative poverty of temporal and modal distinctions of Hebrew verbs, one may feel a bit wistful that this convention was not preserved by later writers.

In any case, these instances just enumerated are no more than local oddities in a prose that, as I have said, seems remarkably modern in its suppleness. One small reflection of its modernity is another traditional term that Gnessin edges into a new acceptation—in this case, in complete agreement with what has come to be standard modern usage. The verbal noun *hakarah*, from the verb *haker* ("to recognize or know"), is here used to designate not recognition, but consciousness: "with confused consciousness he set the glass of water down." The new usage, of course, is motivated by the etymological analogy of the various European languages, which derive the term for consciousness from a root meaning "knowledge": German *Bewusstsein;* French *conscience;* English *consciousness.* I am not sure whether Gnessin is the first to use *hakarah* in this sense, but this would hardly be surprising, given his central expressive need for verbal labels to characterize mental and emotional processes and faculties.[9] Although in contemporary Hebrew *hakarah* as a designation of consciousness has a strong competitor with a slightly different semantic range, *toda'ah,* derived from the other primary Hebrew verb for "knowing," it has been so acclimated in the language in this sense that it is also used with a prefix, *tat-hakarah,* the term for "the subconscious."

The casually achieved rightness of this neologism is an exceptional instance of a pervasive quality of this prose, at least as we read it with historical hindsight: in its diction, in its syntax, in its rhythms, in the inner logic of the formal configurations it assumes, it seems surprisingly *natural* as mimetic literary prose. We are driven back to the question that was our point of departure: how was it possible to do this when the language was not a spoken language? The tentative answer I shall propose involves a consideration of the distinctive literary history of Hebrew as well as the general nature of mimetic language in the kind of fiction bent on the representation of inner states.

We noted at the outset that Hebrew, in continuous literary use for more than three thousand years, has never really been a dead language. I would add that the central texts of rabbinic Hebrew are also a literature filled with living voices. The Mishnah is a written compilation of what was initially an oral study of the law, and it retains, in the very cadences and turns of speech of its questions and responses and conclusions, abundant traces of its oral origins. The midrashim have a prehistory as actual sermons, and in their homey diction and their lively imagery they strive toward a literary recreation of the living immediacy of the preacher addressing his congregation. [10] Thus, the rabbinic classics possess what could be called a vernacular-like character, for all their manifest status as literary texts.

Mendele's rabbinic solution, then, to the problem of making Hebrew work in prose fiction was essential to Gnessin, who had a very different artistic program from that of the master satirist of Jewish life in the Pale of Settlement. Gnessin, by building his language on a matrix of rabbinic Hebrew, though with perfect freedom to introduce other historical components of the language, both early and late, could draw on a whole corpus of precedents, some distant, some direct, for endowing Hebrew with the qualities of living speech. These precedents did not altogether solve the problem of dialogue for him. (Especially now that Hebrew is an ordinary spoken language for three-and-a-half million people, the exchanges between characters in his stories are bound to seem stiff, or a little unreal.) But Gnessin's main emphasis is the unspoken language of inner experience. In this regard, whether he is rendering consciousness as it speaks itself (narrated monologue) or variously summarizing and evoking consciousness in the concert of verbal strategies that constitutes psycho-narration, he is remarkably successful in tapping the vernacular-like elements in classical Hebrew to create a new, realistically persuasive literary vernacular.

Now, the European novel since Stendhal and since Flaubert after him had made rich use of third-person narration for variously fashioning the fictional world from the character's perspective, often with the most subtle simulation of the character's incessant inner movements of thought, sensory perception, memory, and feeling. But when critics say, as I have done, that experiential realism somehow renders the unspoken inner speech of the characters, they partially misrepresent the relation between consciousness and language. Consciousness, as I think we can recognize from introspection, is incipiently and fragmentarily verbal; it is not simply unspoken speech. Joyce's use of elliptical sentences and suppressed logical connections in his stream of consciousness is a strategy of stylization for intimating this incipience. Consciousness may contain citations or simulations of actual speech or of literary discourse, as well as perceptions or recollections that are not cast primarily in verbal form but rather are experienced as images, kinesthetic apprehensions, or *Gestalten* of ideas and sensory data not tied to linguistic formulation. The notion that the language of realism requires a vernacular base is imprecise, for what most novelists do is to weave certain vernacular elements together with manifestly literary strands of language.

This mixture of stylistic means has the capacity to represent almost simultaneously the speechlike elements of consciousness, the verbal traits that consciousness draws from its knowledge of literary texts and literary clichés, and the nonverbal components of consciousness for which the novelistic narrator provides his own voice and language. Here is an exemplary instance of experiential realism from Joseph Conrad's *The Secret Agent,* a novel published in 1907, at the very moment when Gnessin was producing his novellas. Formally, Gnessin is a more radical modernist than Conrad, but they are joined in the enterprise of telling the story through the cogitations and imaginations and pulse beats of the character. Conrad's Mr. Verloc has just jerked up the Venetian blinds to contemplate through the window "the enormity of cold, black, wet, muddy accumulation of bricks, slates, and stones" outside. Looking out windows, we should note, is a characteristic gesture in this and many other novels, and there is a good deal of it in Gnessin, too, for it is an apt emblem of the mind contemplating the world from a fixed viewpoint through a transparent but separating and sometimes distortive medium:

> Mr. Verloc felt the latent unfriendliness of all outdoors with a force approaching to positive bodily anguish. There is no occupation that fails a man more completely than that of a secret agent of the police. It's like your horse suddenly falling dead under you in the midst of an uninhabited and thirsty plain. The comparison occurred to Mr. Verloc because he had sat astride

various army horses in his time, and had now the sensation of an incipient fall. The prospect was as black as the windowpane against which he was leaning his forehead. And suddenly the face of Mr. Vladimir, clean-shaved and witty, appeared enhaloed in the glow of its rosy complexion like a sort of pink seal impressed on the fatal darkness.[11]

The unsignaled transitions from psycho-narration to narrated monologue are typical of experiential realism. Mr. Verloc's feeling the unfriendliness outdoors with a bodily anguish is, no doubt, an account in the narrator's literary diction of an apprehension that is preverbal or nonverbal. Then we are not sure to whom to attribute the aphoristic generalization in the present tense ("there is no occupation that fails a man. . . . It's like your horse suddenly falling") until the narrator supplies the attribution for us ("the comparison occurred to Mr. Verloc"), adding some narrative information about Mr. Verloc's military past. The closer approach to the vernacular of consciousness is suggested by the shift to "you," at once more colloquial and more immediate than the third person. The comparison between the blackness of the prospect and the windowpane is in all likelihood the narrator's verbalization of a dim perception of similitude by the character. Then the description of the hallucination, in which Mr. Verloc sees the face of Mr. Vladimir, his suavely sinister employer from a foreign secret service, in the dark outside the window, is rendered in the narrator's formal language. Note the carefully chosen "enhaloed" and the elaborate, portentous simile, "like a pink seal impressed on the fatal darkness," together with the motifs of clean-shavenness and wit—qualities Mr. Vladimir himself had admired earlier when he glimpsed his own face in a mirror.

The passage from *The Secret Agent* instructively illustrates how this kind of novelistic realism calls on certain vernacular elements ("it's like your horse falling dead under you") in a language that constantly uses more formal diction, more intricately contrived figures of speech and recurrences of motif, for the rendering of the character's experience. If a writer like Gnessin often simulates the confused and fragmentary nature of unfocused thought, he also, like Conrad, frequently uses painstakingly elaborated figurative language to evoke states of consciousness for which consciousness itself has no words. Here is the narrator's brief observation on Hagzar's chronic condition of quiet desperation: "and the heart felt as though some thin crust were peeling off within it, and that thin crust were peeling and splitting and separating into bubbles, little bubbles, and these were sliding out and pressing against the chest and bursting into the throat."[12]

What Gnessin needed, in sum, for the success of his innovative enterprise was not a vernacular but vernacular-like elements that he could incorporate in the wrought textures of a more literary language. Such elements were abundantly available to him in the heritage of rabbinic Hebrew, and the model of Mendele, for all his divergence from it, had shown how that heritage could be exploited. Mendele had managed to make the language of the sages the medium of vividly satiric storytelling, pungent with the concrete details of quotidian reality. Gnessin, reshaping that language to follow the contours of a European syntax and European modes of conceptualization, converted it into the most persuasive expression of inner experience. Nearly two decades before kindergarten children prattled in Hebrew, before politicians made speeches in Hebrew, before vendors hawked their wares in a raucous Hebrew vernacular, Gnessin's literary transformation of the classical language made it a lifelike vehicle for the ebb and flow of consciousness of his hypersensitive, self-subverting, Russian-speaking intellectuals.

# 3

# Realism
# Without
# Vernacular

T he *fin-de-siècle* fashioners of a new Hebrew prose whom we have been considering, with the single exception of Y. H. Brenner, had no part in the Zionist enterprise. They were not necessarily antipathetic to the early stirrings of Zionism in their time, but they themselves were drawn to a different cultural horizon. It is quite possible that there was, nevertheless, a powerful if unintended connection between their peculiar literary project and the political project of Zionism that would gather momentum through the next three or four decades. The Israeli critic Dov Sadan long ago proposed that there was a kind of imaginative logic which produced a compelling movement from literature to politics: after writers had succeeded in creating an "as if" reality in Hebrew, the conditions of consciousness had been established in their readers for seeking to build an actual Hebrew reality, with all the requisite social institutions and political apparatus, in the real geography of this world.[1]

My guess is that Sadan's suggestion contains a kernel of truth neglected in the conventional accounts of the rise of Zionism. It is, however, a truth of hindsight, for what Mendele and his forerunners in the Hebrew Enlightenment had in mind (and—after Mendele—Gnessin, Berdichevsky, and most of their contemporaries) was the creation on Central and Eastern European soil of an authentically European Hebrew fiction. (The proponents of the Hebrew literary revival had similar aspirations for poetry and discursive prose, but fiction provided the crucial test case for their anomalous enterprise because it involved not just expression and argument but the constitution in language of a whole world that could encompass the consciousness of the characters, their speech, their appearance and gestures and dress, and the social institutions and natural settings they inhabited.) To create a body of modern fiction in Hebrew was a way of remaining profoundly Jewish in cultural identity—an identity continuous in language and allusion with the three-thousand-year tradition of Hebrew literature—and at the same time thoroughly at home in the realm of cosmopolitan European culture, exploiting the resources of what had been since the eighteenth century the characteristically modern European genre, the novel. For the handful of intellectuals, spun off from the traditional Jewish milieu, who had forged the new Hebrew fiction, it was in a sense a calling card that gave them entry to the great polyglot salon of European culture, as if to say: We belong here as equals, and we are proud to display our original address.

The strong perception of Hebrew as the living national language of the Jews, even as it remained an unspoken tongue, was a necessary but not a sufficient condition for this literary movement. A cultural setting was also required that could make feasible the very idea of a literary enclave using a language other than that of the majority national group. The extraordinary flowering of Hebrew literature in medieval Spain was made possible in part because the Jews of that time and place had before their eyes in the Arabs a model of a people who spoke one language, vernacular Arabic, and wrote another, the classical Arabic of the Quran; the Jews were thus spurred to competitive imitation, using the classical Hebrew of the Bible. It seems likely that the transplanting of the Iberian Hebrew revival to Renaissance Italy was facilitated because a roughly analogous linguistic situation obtained there: Italy was fragmented by local dialects that were in many instances not even mutually comprehensible, while after Dante the usual medium of literary expression was Tuscan, which was in a way an artificial language, at least from the viewpoint of the other regions.

Modern Hebrew literature, though its ideological beginnings are in monolingual eighteenth-century Prussia, came to fruition chiefly in the multinational, multilingual Russian and Austro-Hungarian empires. In the townlets from which many of the Hebrew writers came, as well as in the various urban centers to which they gravitated, it would not have been unusual for them to have heard spoken by different national-ethnic groups two or three or even four languages—Russian, Polish, Ukrainian, German, Ruthenian, and, of course, Yiddish. Against this background, it would have been far less bizarre for them than it may seem to us to create a body of fiction in which the cafés and parks and reading rooms of Odessa, Vilna, Warsaw, and Vienna are populated by figures that talk and think in Hebrew. When some of the devotees of the Hebrew revival migrated westward, beginning early in this century and in increasing numbers between the two wars, they carried their linguistic reflexes with them to places like Berlin, Paris, London, and New York. But as anyone can attest who has had the opportunity to know the émigré Hebraists in New York as recently as the 1950s, these writers, displaced from their multilingual setting, were doomed to declaim sonorous Hebrew cadences in a historical vacuum. In an essentially monolingual country that offered relatively open access to people of talent, those with literary gifts in the younger generation—as occurred spectacularly with the children of the eastern European Jewish immigration to the United States—would of course be drawn to the dominant language. The older Hebraists, then, were left brandishing a literary torch with no one to whom they could pass it on.

By the first decade of the twentieth century, partly for the reasons specified by Dov Sadan, more and more of the young Hebrew writers were making their way to Palestine. They were attracted by the promise of national renascence of the Second Aliyah, or immigration, which was in fact really the first wave of Zionist immigration to involve more than a tiny handful of pioneers. In those years Hebrew literary works began to be published in the Land of Israel, and the first Hebrew literary journals there made their appearance. Paradigmatic is the story of a nineteen-year-old Hebrew fiction writer named Shmuel Yosef Czaczkes. In 1907 he arrived in Palestine by way of Vienna from his hometown in Galicia at the eastern end of the Austro-Hungarian empire, with the double intention of making his literary career and realizing himself as a Zionist. After six years, the young man, who had

changed his name to Agnon and had already achieved a rather
spectacular early success, felt that the arid cultural atmosphere in
the Palestine of those years was too limiting, and he went to
Germany, apparently with the vague intention (in fact, to be
impressively realized) of extending his self-cultivation as an auto-
didact. Caught in Germany by the outbreak of the First World
War, Agnon remained there until 1924. He became in those years
a major figure in Hebrew fiction and a writer with an economically secure future, having acquired as patron Zalman Schocken,
the German department-store magnate turned publisher. By the
time Agnon returned to Palestine and settled permanently in
Jerusalem, the center of Hebrew literature had shifted decisively
to the Land of Israel, and the revival of Hebrew as a spoken
language (which Agnon himself would always pronounce with a
marked Galician-Yiddish accent) was in full swing.

What complemented this pull toward the ancestral land was
the destruction of the European cultural base of Hebrew literature
in the years 1914 to 1918 and thereafter. The Austro-Hungarian
empire was broken up after the war, in part replaced by a group of
more nearly monolingual national entities that could not provide
so congenial a context for the flourishing of a literature in Hebrew. More decisively, the overthrow of the Czarist regime by the
Soviet revolution rang the death knell on Hebrew literature in its
greatest European center. In the first few years after the revolution, there were some ambiguous grounds for hoping that the
Bolshevik regime might look with favor on Hebrew as a legiti-
mate member of the family of ethnic-linguistic traditions allowed
to continue their development under the Soviet umbrella. Habimah, the first Hebrew repertory theater, was established in 1917
and was allowed (with Stalin's approval!) to continue through the
mid-1920s. Two Hebrew literary miscellanies were published,
featuring poems and stories that rhapsodically praised the revolution as the dawning of a new age of freedom for all mankind. But
very quickly Hebrew was declared a counterrevolutionary "cleri-

cal" language; Hebrew publication was banned, and instruction of the language was prohibited.

One by one the Hebrew writers made their way across the border to the West, aided, in a couple of notable instances, by the intervention of Maxim Gorky, who was acquainted with some of the Hebrew poets and novelists and had influence with Lenin. For a time, during the 1920s, it seemed as though Hebrew literature might be able to establish new European bases, especially in Berlin and Paris. In Germany, two fine Hebrew publishing houses were active, Stybel (transplanted from Moscow via Warsaw) and Schocken (the latter also having a German-language operation), which in the quality of their literary titles and the elegance of their typography and bookbinding would not be surpassed by any of their Israeli successors. *HaTekufah,* one of the most impressive of the European Hebrew literary journals, was issued from Berlin, having migrated westward from Moscow, where it was founded in 1917. In all likelihood, none of this would have sustained itself in the West, with its open invitation to cultural assimilation, for more than a generation, but as European history took a catastrophic turn of unprecedented proportions, 1933 put an abrupt end to Hebrew literature in Germany, and 1939 to Hebrew literature in the rest of Europe.

One of the most fascinating and, finally, exemplary figures in Hebrew literature during these years of gathering darkness is the poet and novelist David Fogel. He was born in a small town in Podolia, in the southwestern Ukraine, in 1891, which places him almost a generation after Gnessin and nearly coeval with Agnon (born 1888). At the age of nineteen, Fogel sets out on what will prove to be a career of incessant peregrinations. He sojourns briefly in Vilna, then Odessa, Lemburg, and, beginning in 1912, in Vienna, as if on an inadvertent pilgrimage of the major way stations of Hebrew literature in Europe. Overtaken in Vienna by the First World War, he is arrested as an alien subject and spends almost two and a half years in prison. Life outside of prison walls is scarcely less bleak: Fogel is constantly at the edge of poverty, supporting himself one hardly knows how, and he lives in relative isolation. His somber modernist poetry, collected in 1923 under the title *Before the Dark Gate* (*Lifnei hasha'ar ha'afel*), generally meets with incomprehension or hostile criticism. His first marriage, in 1919, lasts only four years, and both he and his wife suffer from consumption. In the mid-1920s Fogel moves from Vienna to Paris. Late in 1929 he travels to Palestine with the apparent intention of settling there, but this quintessential European feels himself an outsider to the new Zionist reality in the Middle East. After a few months he returns to Europe, to another year of restless movement; then in 1931, back to Paris, where he remarries and has a daughter. From the late 1920s onward, he concentrates on fiction, writing a novella, *Sanitarium* (*Beit marpei'*, 1927), publishing with a house in Palestine a fascinating novel of psychological aberration, *Married Life* (*Hayei nisu'im*, 1929–1930), and then, in 1932, another novella, *Facing the Sea* (*Nokhah hayam*). He is caught in France by the Nazi invasion; the last that is known of him is an indication in an official document that he was "transported" to Germany in February 1944—into the kingdom of death.

The best one can say of this melancholy tale is that it has a posthumous happy ending. Until the early 1960s Fogel was usually thought of as a peripheral figure in Hebrew literature. In 1966 the prominent Israeli poet Dan Pagis edited and introduced *The Complete Poetry of David Fogel* (*Kol shirei David Fogel*). Many younger Hebrew critics and poets now began to view Fogel, with his understatement, his ellipses and dissonances, his imagistic and expressionistic qualities, as a major precursor of post-1948 poetic modernism in Hebrew. His novella *Facing the Sea,* originally published only in periodical form, was rediscovered and reissued in 1974 as an elegant little volume by the prestigious Siman Keriah Publishers. And the same house has brought out (1987) a new edition of *Married Life,* with significant revisions based on the original manuscript buried by Fogel in a garden in Paris before his last arrest and eventually conveyed to Israel.

*Facing the Sea* provides an apt epilogue to the story of the invention of Hebrew prose on European ground. It was composed, as I have noted, in 1932, at the last moment before the curtain of apocalypse began to come down on European civilization. Its setting and subject are preeminently European. Adolph Barth, a Viennese engineer with a job in Paris, comes with his lovely young mistress Gina, also Viennese, for a summer's vacation to a little seaside town on the Riviera a few miles from Nice. Under the baking sun, in the seminakedness of bathing costumes—"Nakedness banished the distance between them, leveled them to the fundamental equality of the hour of birth and death"—multiple entanglements ensue. Barth has a single, passionately fierce sexual encounter with a French woman named Marcelle. Gina attracts but wards off a German named Kraft, whom she meets on an expedition to Nice. Then she succumbs, letting her will go slack and her body take over, to a certain Cici, a swarthy, powerful, sexually insistent Italian workman. Afterward, she undergoes an extreme reflex of revulsion, as much from her own body, which she feels has asserted a kind of alien independence, as from her seducer. The experience, with its manifestation of a primal erotic urge that is essentially impersonal, as indifferent to emotional attachments as to propriety, taints her relationship with Barth. In the end she insists on leaving him. The last image of the novella is her receding view, from the window of her northward-bound train, of Barth standing on the platform "like a lifeless beam, his head leaning slightly to one side, holding his hat with an upraised hand, without waving it."

I have outlined the plot of *Facing the Sea* in part to suggest how thoroughly European, and how thoroughly characteristic of the period between the two wars, this novella is. The vacation setting involves a coming together of figures from different points on the European map, and, despite the Hebrew medium, there is no indication that any of the characters is a Jew. Unlike another branch of Hebrew literature, which constantly revolves around a problematic of Jewish national and historical concerns, the themes of this story are as universal as eros and civilization. The disruptive sexual magnetism of the dark, southern, working-class male felt by the northern European woman is a subject familiar to readers of English literature from the stories of D. H. Lawrence. The use of the holiday situation, on the edge of the elemental sea, as an occasion for the dissolution of customary barriers, the release of dark urges (there is a hint of animalistic violence in the sexual acts; the nightlife of the vacationers, complete with naked dancing, is orgiastic; and Cici ends up knifing someone in an argument), all this is reminiscent of Thomas Mann, some of Nabokov's 1930s stories, and other fiction of this period. I'm not sure if enough is known about Fogel's actual reading to propose influences, but the affinities in theme and setting with a broad current of twentieth-century European fiction are striking.

What concerns us centrally is the degree to which Fogel succeeds in realizing these themes and this story in a language that, unlike Mann's German, Lawrence's English, and Nabokov's Russian, was not a spoken language. By 1932 Hebrew had, in fact, become a spoken language in Palestine, but as far as Fogel was concerned, it was not a vernacular. He was no doubt in touch through reading with new coinages and other kinds of innovation of the revived Hebrew of the Land of Israel, and, even without his brief stay there, he would certainly have been capable of sustaining a conversation in Hebrew. Nevertheless, his Hebrew came to him through literary sources and has the earmarks of a literary language without a vernacular base. This characteristic is transparently evident in his stilted, artificial dialogue, which is compounded of phrases from classical texts and bears little relation to Hebrew as it was spoken even in 1932.

Given the inadvertent quaintness of the language of the dialogues, the great surprise about the prose of Fogel's narrator is that it is so unarchaic, so supple and precise. Here and there, to be sure, there are certain odd terms for particular garments or objects that have not become part of modern Hebrew usage: it's a bit like reading a contemporary story by E. M. Forster or Katherine Mansfield and occasionally running into a Middle English word for *robe* or *slip* or *balcony*. But these are no more than minor moments of strangeness in a mimetic prose that is more fluent, even more beautifully *natural,* than anything that would be produced in the next generation—the first native one—of Hebrew fiction in Israel after 1948. The potential for artistic maturity in the European tradition of Hebrew writing may be suggested by the fact that Fogel's stylistic achievement would be matched, or surpassed, only in the second and third generations of native Israeli fiction, in the work of writers like Amalia Kahana-Carmon, the later A. B. Yehoshua, Yaakov Shabtai, Yitzhak Ben-Ner, and, most recently, David Grossman.

In tracing the transition from Mendele to Gnessin and other anti-*nusakh* writers in the early years of the century, I have placed considerable stress on the newly central role accorded to representing states of consciousness. Bits of narrated monologue and even quoted interior monologue appear in Fogel, and one suspects his prose would not have the suppleness it does without the example of Gnessin. But on the whole Fogel is much less interested in the direct representation of consciousness in its own idiom than in the narratorial mediation of consciousness. This report of consciousness in turn is integrated with the rendering of scene and action in a language, belonging to the narrator, which at once has lyric suggestiveness and painterly precision. For Gnessin, absorbed in mental process, the proper subject of fiction is the inner world of feeling, cogitation, and recollection, for which the external world is no more than pretext or stimulus. Fogel, on the other hand, is constantly drawn by the allure of the outward reality accessible to sensory perception; as a result, he repeatedly strives for a coherent visual definition of scene, seeking to appropriate the sensory world through his Hebrew with the same poised authority that one might find in the French of Gide and Proust, or the German of Musil and Broch. In his prose as in his poetry, Fogel is always wary of the habits of effusion that have marred much modern Hebrew writing, and so these acts of mimetic appropriation are for the most part carried out with a few carefully controlled strokes. Here, for example, is Fogel's representation of a midsummer noon in the little Riviera town. Gina and Barth have just returned from swimming and are preparing to go into the local restaurant for lunch:

> The sun now stood directly overhead. In the main street, made up of a single row of houses facing the sea, as though split lengthwise, the lights shimmered like molten orange liquid. The solitary passersby crushed their own shadows beneath their feet.[2]

I have called the narrator's language painterly, but one must add that the painterly quality has a decidedly postimpressionist cast, exhibiting in the novella as a whole a preference for a few bold primary colors—orange, blue, yellow, and an occasional red. Figurative language, though it plays an important role in conveying the nuances of sensory detail as well as the mood of the scene, is compact to the point of terseness, in keeping with the scaled-down proportions of the whole description: the play of lights is "like molten orange liquid," and the pedestrians in this relentless noonday brilliance appear to be crushing or trampling their own foreshortened shadows. In translation, all this may seem deft if unexceptional writing. Reading it in the original, one is struck by the extraordinary precision of the diction. The words are all available to the writer from the classical Hebrew sources, both biblical and rabbinic (Fogel is not especially inclined to neologisms); but after two generations of post-Haskalah prose, which had shown how this old wine could be poured into new bottles of various shapes and sizes, Fogel is able to make the classical vocabulary work with the nicety of a living literary language, sure of the fine shadings of meaning and the range of associations of different terms.

The ultimate lexical origins of the first sentence, "The sun now stood directly overhead," are biblical. The phrase does not seem particularly biblical even in the Hebrew—in contrast with the inset of allusion or mock-epic style in *nusakh* prose—but rather is felt as a telling report of simple temporal information. In the original, the sun does not "stand" but, in good Hebraic idiom, "encamps." What I have rendered as "overhead" is literally "on the head," with the word for "head" not the standard *ro'sh* but *qodqod,* a term that, quite shorn of the many figurative senses attached to *ro'sh,* better conveys the sheer physicality of this part of the body, its very skullness. (*Qodqod,* by this time, also had the geometric sense of "angle," as in a triangle, and if Fogel had this association in mind, the term might be meant to convey a cubist effect.)³ Thus through the most minimal verbal gesture, Fogel's narrator beautifully communicates a sense of the sun at its fierce zenith pounding down on the exposed human head, encamped over or on it.

The more conspicuously poetic move of representing the shimmer of reflected lights as molten orange liquid is a more intricate instance of impressive lexical precision in the Hebrew. The verb for "shimmer" (*rahash*) has a basic meaning of minute oscillating movement and a semantic range that could include swarming, stirring, seething, vibrating, even buzzing; it is exactly the right choice for the hazy, trembling movement of summer sunlight over surfaces. Of half a dozen or more Hebrew words for burning hot or "molten," the one selected, *lohet,* is perfect for the descriptive task at hand because it suggests incandescence and brilliance and is also cognate with a term that means passion. Finally, the rather ordinary "lights" of my English version is, in the original, not the standard *'orot* but the distinctly literary *negohot* (in the Bible used only in poetry). In context, the term has an aestheticizing effect: it is not a simple variation of light that the narrator's eye detects in the noonday scene but a play of luminosities, a spectrum of effulgences in orange-hot fluid incandescence.

What I have been describing in these few lines, and what is pervasive in the style of *Facing the Sea,* is a sense communicated by

the language of the writer's having unlocked the expressive resources of classical Hebrew to fulfill the aims of a thoroughly
European fictional realism. As a matter of historical linguistics, it
is noteworthy that by 1932 a consensus of literary usage involving
nuanced distinctions among terms had crystallized. It is true that
in the realm of material existence, in the vocabulary for foods and
implements and apparel, there were still elements of instability
and vagueness. These would be settled only as full agreement on
meanings emerged from the one place where Hebrew was being
used as the spoken and written language of everyday life. But
Fogel's prose is striking testimony to this early consensus of
literary usage; his ability to work assuredly within the consensus
explains to a large extent why much of his language continues to
seem contemporary.

Let me offer just one more example, this time with briefer
commentary, of Fogel's descriptive precision—a water scene to
match the land scene we have just looked at:

> The water beat secretly against the beach. Nearby a rowboat
> crept past filled with naked bodies, noise, and laughter. Stefano's
> brood were in it, Marcelle and her Parisian girlfriend, too. Arms
> and legs dangled over the sides of the boat and splashed through
> the water. From amongst the voices peered the heavy, orange
> stillness.[4]

The scene is realized not from the angle of perception of any
of the characters but from the overviewing standpoint of the
narrator, who is content, however, to suggest the objects of
description fragmentarily—in rhetorical terms, by synecdoche,
the part for the whole: naked bodies, a tangle of protruding
limbs, a confusion of voices and laughter. (We have already
noted the fondness for synecdoche in Gnessin.) Again, the Hebrew moves with the assurance of lexical authority: *nithabtu,* a
passive-reflexive form (essentially used as a "middle voice" for
agentless action), nicely appropriate for the beating or slapping
of the waves against the shore; *meshurbavot* for the arms and legs,

a word that means "to stick out" and/or "to dangle"; *nishtakh-shekhu* for the splashing of the limbs in the water, another rabbinic passive-reflexive verb form, using a root that is associated with rinsing or laundering and rapid to-and-fro movement, and that in context produces an onomatopoeic effect. Capping this descriptive fidelity, Fogel suggests the mood, the "inscape," of the scene, by shifting to a more explicitly poetic strategy, synesthesia and metaphor, as the stillness, heavy and orange, is made to peer or peep out (*heitsitsah*) from the midst of the thicket of sound. The paradox of silence—a palpable, colored silence—hiding at the heart of noise and laughter is characteristic of Fogel's rendering of this whole holiday world, in which the revelry of the vacationers is played out within a force field of impersonal powers, disturbing in their implacability.

This troubling vision of the fragility, the quite literal superficiality, of civilized reality is central to our general concerns. The creation of a new Hebrew prose involved much more than the shaping of a linguistic instrument to answer technical needs of representation: states of consciousness, physical appearance, mechanical procedures, material objects, and so forth. Writing novels in Hebrew, as we have noted, was intertwined with the adoption of a European mind-set in regard to such fundamental aspects of the conceptual world as the indication of causation, relation, and association; the discrimination of time; the perception of sensory details and their importance; and the spatial definition of action. But beyond such epistemological categories, modern Hebrew writers—perhaps more radically in prose fiction than in poetry—were embarked on what was in effect a transvaluation of Jewish values, whether they happened to be Nietzschean, like Berdichevsky, or nonideological, like Fogel, or even seemingly traditionalist, like Agnon. In most instances, including the one we are scrutinizing, this transvaluation was not the consequence of a willed effort to stand the world of classical Judaism on its head. Rather it was the inevitable reflection of a process of acculturation in depth. The Hebrew writers, nurtured on the imagina-

tive and philosophic literature of modern Europe, very often came
to see the world in a perspective sharply different from that of
their forebears, and they were impelled to make their language
match that new vision.

I do not mean to suggest that the classical Jewish sources
themselves exhibit anything dimly resembling unanimity in their
implied sense of what the world is like; in fact, the historical
spectrum that runs from the Bible to rabbinic literature to medieval philosophy and the Kabbalah is altogether baffling in its
variety. There are nevertheless certain notions, certain modes of
conceptualization which remain outside the range of this varied
tradition that would exert powerful appeal on the modern Hebrew imagination. Two such notions are of central relevance to
*Facing the Sea:* the precarious status of civilization over against a
more enduring world of elemental forces; and the related idea of a
split between mind and body, in which body is not the *yetser* of
rabbinic literature, the instinctual urge that is an energizer of the
soul, but is instead a weirdly autonomous entity, vaguely threat-
ening to consciousness. How does Fogel go about conveying this
new, manifestly disorienting sense of reality?

Technically, the stance of his narrator, enjoying free access to
the consciousness of the characters from a viewpoint that remains
outside—or perhaps above—consciousness, with the freedom to
depict it analytically, is indispensable for the imaginative definition of the writer's distinctive vision. Let me offer two examples
of this careful refraction of the inner life of the characters through
the narrator's language—a relatively simple one from early in the
novella, and a more complex, summarizing instance that appears
just before the end. When Gina goes off by herself on a day's
outing to Nice, she is described as exuding a kind of sensual
ripeness in her strawberry-red silk dress and her big earrings,
stirring fantasies—the narrator's or those of the men who see
her?—of exotic lands "where people go around naked and their
heart's impulse is wild and mighty, rooted in primeval nature, in

God." In this ambiance of generalized arousal, in the scorching midsummer heat, she sits down at a sidewalk cafe:

> Leaning back, she took pleasure in this idle sitting at the edge of the noisy boulevard. She looked at the people, scrutinized the faces of the women and what they were wearing, and the day burned hotter and hotter before her eyes. The pulse of life pounded fiercely, within her as outside her. The sensation of her own body was awake in her, and she felt affection for it, for this mysterious seething body, as for a creature distinct from her.[5]

This moment nicely illustrates how Fogel is able to move from the experiential realism pioneered in Hebrew by Gnessin to the narrative representation of what amounts to a new ontology. The depiction of a pretty young woman, alone in a Riviera resort town, checking out the looks and clothes of the women going by, has an obvious realistic plausibility. The pivotal point in the passage, I think, is the little clause, "and the day burned hotter and hotter before her eyes," which in the Hebrew is more compact and more graceful, if in one respect a bit odd: *vehayom lahat le'eynehah vehalakh.* The tense used is a progressive form derived from rabbinic Hebrew (*pa'al vehalakh*) which is used to indicate a steady intensification of the action specified by the verb. The utilization of the form here is perfectly continuous with the interest in subjectively experienced process that we observed in Gnessin. The slight oddness is that the Hebrew *le'eynehah* ("before her eyes") is inserted, against the grain of the idiom, between the verb ("burned hot," "glowed") and the intensifying auxiliary, *halakh.* This small syntactic maneuver has the effect of stressing the subjectivity of the perception: the day is no doubt hot, but it is through Gina's eyes as she sits in the café that the shimmering waves of mounting heat are seen. The next sentence, however, firmly ties what is going on within her to what is going on in the world around her. Its grammatical and thematic subject, "the pulse of life" (*dofeq haḥayim*), is no doubt a European collocation;

it is just the sort of phrase that Berdichevsky, with his revisionist vitalism, might have imported into Hebrew, though I cannot document that in this case. The notion of an intersubjective and perhaps cosmic "pulse of life" is not one that occurs in the various currents of traditional Jewish thought, but in Fogel's novella the whole plot ultimately turns on that idea. Once it has been introduced here, pounding both within the protagonist and outside her, the narrator proceeds with a complex definition of the nature of her consciousness at this moment, as she feels affection for her body, which seems to her strangely disjunct and not a natural extension of her sense of self.

As I intimated before, this is not a state of mind, or of mind/body, for which classical Hebrew has a conceptual vocabulary. Fogel depends crucially on the modern coinage *tehushah* ("sensation," from the verb *hush*, "to feel") because this sort of discrimination needs a vocabulary that will give it a power of nice abstraction. The concluding adjective *badul* ("distinct" or "separate") is a rabbinic term that is given a specialized modern meaning; it thus complements "sensation" in making possible the analytic precision of the observation.

Otherwise, what happens stylistically is that Fogel pushes indigenous Hebrew idioms to convey unfamiliar perceptions and relations. Symptomatically, Gina feels affection for her body, *hagtah 'elav 'ahavah*, a phrase based on the rabbinic *hagah 'elav hibah*, though probably a shade stronger, as *'ahavah*, in distinction to *hibah*, is more like love than affection. The idiom sounds perfectly natural in Hebrew, but the context is surprising, even disorienting, for in the midrashic texts where the usage originates, nobody is ever said to feel affection for his or her own body. It is a small instance of how a strange new world is constituted in the words of an age-old Hebrew.

Toward the end of the novella, after Gina has announced to Barth her intention to leave him, at least for the time being, he steps out onto the balcony of their hotel room, looking back on her as she packs her suitcase. In this instance, as the narrator

moves into the consciousness of the character, he employs more
elaborately metaphorical means:

> He arose and walked over to the balcony door, then stood there
> facing into the room. Silently he followed her movements. From
> outside, the muted sound of piano playing filtered in, no doubt
> from the nearby *pension*. And this playing, too, was now unfamil-
> iar, not a part of the necklace of shining days and nights, colored
> with sun and moon, but the opposite: alien, infuriating, like a
> foreign element that didn't belong here. Here there was no place
> now for a spirit of gentle and delicate nocturnal melancholy that is
> absorbed by the soul unwittingly and suffuses it like the distant,
> untroubling fragrance of violets. Now, in this space, fragments
> were rolling about of something that had shattered irrevocably,
> neither through his fault nor through Gina's, that had shattered
> through fate's cruelty—and a feeling of orphanhood gnawed and
> pierced to the point of tears.[6]

The two short sentences at the beginning of the paragraph
simply report Barth's physical actions. The third sentence, which
registers the sound of piano playing from the neighboring *pension,*
shifts to the character's point of view. The transition is signaled
by the adverbial indication of supposition, "no doubt" (or, "one
could assume," *mistama'*),[7] instead of the certainty of the omniscient narrator. But what follows is not really narrated monologue, despite a certain contamination, which we shall consider
momentarily, of the narrator's language by the unspoken language of the character. Fogel, in keeping with his general purpose
of intimating experiential process through finely wrought artifice, in a way combining the aims of the *nusakh* and anti-*nusakh*
traditions of Hebrew prose, lends Barth a coherence of metaphoric
summary of experience that is surely more the narrator's than the
character's: the weeks of vacation splendor that have collapsed
into a private nightmare are a "necklace of shining days and
nights, colored with sun and moon," and the broken bond between Barth and Gina is a hopeless heap of fragments rolling
about the room.

Embedded in this poetic and essentially narratorial rendering
of consciousness are bits of citation—"fate's cruelty" at the end,
and, more elaborately, the "spirit of gentle and delicate nocturnal
melancholy" (*ruaḥ shel tugah ʿaravit qalilah vaʿanugah*) that Barth
feels has vanished from the space he shares with Gina. The phrase
reflects a certain banal sentimental lyricism in the character, who
is an engineer by training but presumably possesses a degree of
Central European high-middlebrow literary cultivation. Stylistically, the language here echoes the Hebrew lyric poetry in vogue
in the late Haskalah through the 1890s and beyond, roughly
equivalent in its aestheticizing effusions to pre-Raphaelite verse
in English. Fogel's use of the citation illustrates how modern
Hebrew had managed to become a multilayered literary language
well before it was revived as a vernacular. Stylistic precedents give
the writer not only a language to represent consciousness but also
to represent, with a suggestion of irony, false consciousness de-
luded by the clichés of popular literature. But the irony is rich
because, like Flaubert's in relation to Emma's romantic raptures
in *Madam Bovary,* it exhibits a certain nostalgic sympathy with
the character's poetic illusions. Thus, Fogel weaves together with
the clichés about nocturnal melancholy his own lyric coinage for
the soul's being suffused by sadness, "like the distant, un-
troubling fragrance of violets." Thus, he gives a suggestion of
genuine delicacy to that poetry-induced condition of lover's
mooniness, the loss of which Barth mourns. This seamless prose,
in sum, enables the writer at once to define the complex meanings
of the character's experience and to indicate a duality of attitudes
toward it.

A final extended illustration will amplify the sense we have
developed of the novelistic ripeness of Fogel's language. It is
the most crucial moment in the plot of *Facing the Sea,* when
Gina gives herself to Cici. The disorienting separation of body
from mind that we noted earlier reaches its thematic climax
here, and Fogel's technical ability to convey this split as a
datum of Gina's consciousness is worth attending to. After

having rebuffed the Italian, she finally agrees to go on a night walk with him:

> When they turned down the dark and narrow path, lined by hedges of scrub that scratched against their legs, Cici looped his arm through hers. A slight trembling went through her at the touch of his arm. But she let him do it. They continued in silence. Only Cici's breathing now was heavy, irregular, audible. Gina felt uneasy. His evident excitement was communicating itself to her, was beginning imperceptibly to master her inward self. What had happened to her all of a sudden?! Her limbs were invaded by a strange exhaustion, a kind of paralysis; walking became difficult for her. A sort of animal stupor filled her that veiled her mind in fog, like the heavy numbness after drinking strong liquor. The pressure of his muscular arm was obscurely felt by her, as though at a certain distance from the zone of her being. The rugged path, jutting with broken stone, she barely saw. She went on like a sleepwalker.
>
> They reached a little clearing. The narrow brook alongside it poured a faint murmur into the body of stillness. In a far-off corner of Gina's soul there flickered a feeling that she had always been walking on this path, that she would continue to walk on it till the end of days, bound up with the delicate murmur and the fragrant night and even with this alien man. It seemed as though all her past life had been drawn out of her and the possibility of her future life as well.
>
> Unconsciously, she sank down on the slope of the brook's channel. And Cici was there sprawled at her feet, whispering in a hot breath unintelligible words. No, Gina understood nothing. She sensed only that her body was burning as though wracked by a high fever. And Cici's searing, biting kisses, on her hands, her bared arms, her neck, her face. The kisses had in them something of the pounce of a terrible beast, of murder. She did not try to protest, she was not capable; and had he intended to kill her, she would not have protested. Again she had no control over herself. She vaguely felt that something was being done in her body, something at once terrible and the source of killing pleasure—but all of it as in a nightmare, as an irrevocable, irresistible decree.[8]

Especially because this moment recalls so many analogues in European literature—English readers will most naturally think of

D. H. Lawrence, both in regard to the situation and the kind of language used to convey it—Fogel's achievement as Hebrew stylist is not adequately represented by the translation. In the half century since these paragraphs were composed, the Hebrew language has in most respects undergone changes at least as extensive, perhaps, as those undergone by English and French since the seventeenth century. Nonetheless, this prose seems remarkably contemporary, as though its author had created, back in 1932, a matrix for standard novelistic diction in Hebrew.

In fact, that creation, as all of our readings have been intended to show, was a collective enterprise, not the work of one writer. The critically formative period ran roughly from 1886 to 1930. Fogel is able to move with such assurance because he can draw on the stylistic achievements and lexical innovations of others as well as on a certain solidification of general usage when he makes his own fine stylistic synthesis. Some of this assurance is observable in mechanical details that would be taken for granted in the literary use of a normal spoken language. Fogel knows, for example, exactly the right idiomatic Hebrew (the verb *shilev*) for someone's slipping his arm inside another person's arm—a usage that Gnessin, three decades earlier, in a passage considered above (see chapter 2, page 62) did not have under control. The external features of the scene, rapidly sketched in accordance with the prevailing economy of report in the novella, are all admirably precise—the scratchy hedge of scrub growth along the narrow path; the rocky, uneven surface; the quiet susurration or "faint murmur" (*mashaq tsanuʿa*) of the brook.

I proposed earlier that, despite the immense differences among individual novelists, there is a prevalent generic way of talking and thinking which might be thought of as standard novelistic, at least for a good part of the realist tradition from the eighteenth century onward. One characteristic of this generic lingua franca would be a fondness for shuttling between the concretely specific details of physical reality and the experiencing mind on which they impinge, which variously feels itself or finds itself in them. Especially when erotic experience is at issue, this shuttling movement is often given a triadic structure, as in our passage from *Facing the Sea:* external reality, inward state, and the body of the human subject, which serves as a threshold between the two. Fogel's emphasis falls on the last two of these three elements, and the vocabulary he calls on for rendering them is rich and precise. He catches the changing nuances of the woman's kinesthetic apprehension of the man at her side: the trembling that runs through her at the touch of his arm, the strange sense of fatigue or numbness that spreads through her limbs, the feeling of feverish body heat, and the progressive dissociation of physical sensation from volitional perception (as when the pressure of Cici's arm is, in the passive voice, "obscurely felt by her," *hurgeshah lah besatum*).

What gives the whole passage psychological density is the writer's ability to provide, in conjunction with this rendering of the body as it undergoes experience, a kind of analytic narration of consciousness. Fogel introduces a few fragments of narrated monologue: "What had happened to her all of a sudden?"; "No, Gina understood nothing"; and perhaps, "had he intended to kill her, she would not have protested." The burden of the scene, however, is carried by a highly mediated version of consciousness, the narrator providing language that would not be available to Gina herself. In some instances this involves the report of ideas or images that clearly occur to her: her fantasy of walking on the narrow path forever, entangled in night and sound and man; her masochistic glimpse into the abyss of sadistic-aggressive male sexuality in the image of the terrible pouncing beast, the intimation of murder. At other points, a strategic role is played by the narrator's nice control of metaphor for the representation of her inner state, as in the animal stupor, recalling the numbing effect of strong drink, that clouds her consciousness.

In executing this complex moment of psycho-narration, Fogel is able to utilize a whole spectrum of finely shaded terms for different inner states or aspects of the self, not all of which, I'm afraid, are effectively represented in my translation. His success, in other words, is equally a testimony to his own artistic gift and to the general maturation of modern Hebrew by the time he wrote. Thus, Cici's condition of excitement masters, or conquers, Gina's "inward self" (*yeshut*), an abstraction that means something like "essence" (literally, "is-ness"), first coined for the purposes of medieval Hebrew philosophy and here used in a sense that straddles the metaphysical and the psychological. Then it is her "mind" (*da'at*) that becomes veiled in fog, a standard Hebrew term that goes all the way back to the Bible and is particularly associated with the cognitive aspect of consciousness and, in several common idioms, with sanity.

Feelings at this point begin to be apprehended obscurely, obliquely, at a certain distance from what I have translated rather literally as "the zone of her being." This last term, *havayah,* the most comprehensive that Fogel employs for the self, is a verbal noun from the root "to be," first used in rabbinic sources in the sense of "that which is" and typically used by modern writers to mean something like "essential being" or "fundamental ontological state." Through this progression of terms, then, Fogel traces the successive stages of a cleavage in the character between being and experience. The new world of experience has terrors—and pleasures—unassimilable by the conscious mind and the concepts of identity by which it sustains itself. Gina's weirdly dissociated perception, at the end, of the sexual act as "something that was being done in [or *to*] her body" culminates this whole development and carries a terrific force of psychological conviction. It becomes clear how the language has been imaginatively redeployed so that it is able to convey a vision of self and world beyond the purview of classical Hebrew culture.

In view of the argument I have been making for the psychological persuasiveness of the passage, and of Fogel's prose in general, a word of explanation should be offered about what may seem, out of context, like a tendentious sexual ideology masquerading as realism. The paralyzing effect on Gina of Cici's aroused maleness may strike some readers as a male writer's self-soothing fantasy of

how a woman should respond to a man, analogous to moments in
D. H. Lawrence or Norman Mailer. In fact, Fogel assumes no
such polarization of passive and active roles between the sexes.
What chiefly intrests him is the potential for the loss of civilized
control in either sex. Earlier in the novella, in Barth's sexual
encounter with Marcelle, it is she who is the aggressor, the one
who is described as a pouncing beast. And in the novel *Married
Life,* the reversal of supposedly traditional sexual roles could
scarcely be more complete: from the first meeting of the couple,
the man—a pale, diminutive intellectual, and a Jew besides—is
the masochist, yielding to the physical and psychological assaults
of the towering blonde "Brunhilde" (an impoverished young Aus-
trian countess), who brutally seizes hold of his life. Fogel, a writer
with no special cause to plead, is repeatedly fascinated by the dark
side of our erotic nature. He patiently mines the resources of
literary Hebrew for the vocabulary, the syntax, the rhythms, the
imagery to probe that darkness through the representation of
fictional lives.

In one respect it may be misleading to think, as we have been
doing, of Fogel's case as the exceptional working out of a cultural
hypothesis that was cut off by subsequent history. Literary Hebrew, it would seem, was already in a rapid process of "normaliza-
tion" during Fogel's own lifetime, like Jewish existence itself, in
the national homeland. The stylistic fumblings, however, and the
painful artificialities of the prose produced by the first generation
of native Hebrew writers, who came of age in the 1940s, would
suggest that the move from vernacular to literary language was by
no means a simple or "natural" one;[9] and, for a variety of historical reasons, it may have been more complicated in Hebrew than
in many other languages. It is surely instructive that Hebrew
literary prose of the 1970s and 1980s would begin to sound more
like Fogel than like the prose of its immediate forebears, the
writers of the Generation of 1948.

The project of creating an authentically European fiction in
Hebrew without a national context and without a vernacular base

was surely anomalous. But it bore witness both to the resources of
expression inherent in the language and to the uncanny binding
force of the language as a medium of cultural identity, beyond
religion and beyond any kind of political nationalism. To make
Hebrew think in a radically new way was what the rabbis, two
millennia earlier, under the pressures of Aramaic, Greek, Latin,
and a transformed social-political world, had done with biblical
Hebrew; and what, a thousand years later, in very different direc-
tions, the great medieval poets and the Jewish philosophers or
their Hebrew translators did, under the pressures of Arabic language and literature and Greek thought. To be sure, these earlier
historical transitions took place when most Jews still lived in
distinct, internally coherent cultural enclaves within the dominant culture; in this regard, the transition into modernity has
been far more disjunctive.

There were of course broader roads than Hebrew that Jews
could take into modernity, whether by ridding themselves of
most of the baggage, linguistic or otherwise, of Jewish tradition,
or by embracing the Yiddish vernacular as the instrument of
modern identity. Only Hebrew, however, satisfied the desire to
preserve continuity with three thousand years of national and
literary experience. To make it into an instrument for the representation of a reality where no living Hebrew voices really spoke
was surely to work against the grain, but perhaps all literary use
of language, however strong the illusion of mimesis, involves
more working against the grain of ordinary language than we are
willing to admit.

Fogel, Gnessin, Berdichevsky, Brenner, and Mendele made it
possible to imagine the world in Hebrew—even as they preserved
many of the language's historical resonances—in terms more radically new than those of any modern Jewish ideology or theology;
they made it possible to conceive of men and women, mind and
matter, individual and society, moment and memory, in a whole
new set of perspectives. Like all fiction writers, they offered no
solutions to the problems of existence, only the imaginative and

linguistic means for thinking about the problems, for seeing them with a depth of vision. The Hebrew movement has never been more than an embattled elite, but for the profundity of its immersion in modernity while holding on to a lifeline to the past, future generations of Jews will continue to be in its debt.

# Epilogue: Language and Literary Realism

It is often true in cultural history that the extreme case may tell us more about a general phenomenon than the run-of-the-mill instance, in which the presumed familiarity of features tends to confirm our preconceptions and keep us from looking below the surface. Thus the Russian Formalist, Victor Shklovsky, in a famous critical provocation, once announced that *Tristram Shandy* was the "the most typical novel of world literature,"[1] . . . which, in an odd but instructive sense, it is, if you begin to recognize that behind the impression of immediacy of even the most persuasively realistic novels inevitably stands an intricate apparatus of artifice and convention.

I am not going to claim that Hebrew literature in Europe is the most typical of modern literatures, but I do think that its striking success in creating a mimetic prose for realistic fiction without the benefit of a spoken language suggests something about how literary language, in general, produces the illusion of realism. That success, of course, could not have been attained without the distinctive resources of the Hebrew that the writers inherited—in particular, as I have tried to explain in my chapters on Mendele and Gnessin, the rich historical layering of the language and the vernacular-like aspects of rabbinic Hebrew. But in other respects, the forging of a language for literary realism has involved the same dynamic for the Hebrew writers that it has for Fielding, Hawthorne, Diderot, and Flaubert.

I have spoken just now, as earlier in this study, of "mimetic" prose, but that is a shorthand term which begs an essential question, for if mimesis is the imitation of reality, it is by no means clear what nonliterary *language* is being imitated in mimetic prose. One influential theory of the novel proposes that makers of the new genre achieved the effect of realism by adopting, as models of imitation, uses of language until then thought to lie below the threshold of literature: diaries, memoirs, personal correspondence, legal depositions, public records, and, above all, the

everyday speech of ordinary people. If this were the whole story of
the language of realism, the invention of Hebrew prose could
never have succeeded, for there were scant Hebrew equivalents for
some of these kinds of discourse, and none at all for the last,
crucial category. In fact, these various borrowings from the vernacular have always been intermittent, and have always involved
not just imitation but an elaborate literary *filtering* of nonliterary
language.

The emergence of the novel in eighteenth-century England is a
case in point. Defoe's *Moll Flanders* is an approximation of the
form and language of a real memoir, the woman's story being
"Written from her own Memorandums," as the title page an-
nounces; but the fictitious editor admits at the beginning of his
Preface that it has been necessary to change Moll's language, for
reasons of decorum, as he says, and also, I would add, to create
the coherent and convincing medium of a literary narrative: "The
original of this story is put into new words, and the stile of the
famous lady we here speak of is a little alter'd, particularly she is
made to tell her own tale in modester words than she told it at
first." Decorums change, but not the need to recast ordinary
language in order to give it expressive coherence: the language of
the narrator in Norman Mailer's *Why Are We in Vietnam?* is more
rather than less obscene than the likely talk of a real-life equivalent, because Mailer keys the rhetoric of his novel on obscenity,
tries to make it work as a kind of poetry.

To return to the genre's eighteenth-century point of departure,
Richardson's epistolary novels, though they do contain elements
of homespun English, are full of strategies of rhetorical heightening—theatrical flourishes, echoes of Milton, the Cavalier poets,
and the King James Version of the Bible: only as we are taken in
by the global illusion of reality produced by the fiction do we
allow ourselves to believe, while we are immersed in the reading
experience, that eighteenth-century English people wrote their
letters in such a language. The purportedly autobiographical
prose of Sterne's *Tristram Shandy* is a stylistic crazy quilt in which

the patches of colloquial language are interstitched with arcane scholastic diction, borrowings and parodies of sundry Renaissance essayists from Burton and Browne onward, snippets of Restoration comedy—all deployed in the extreme stylization of a constant lateral skid of syntax that is partly Sterne's representation of the Lockean "association of ideas," partly a nonstop performance of verbal clowning. Finally, Fielding keeps a coy distance from the actual verbal texture of quotidian experience through his highfalutin diction, his elegantly ironic periods, his mock-epic flights—and none of this prevents his being one of the founders of the realist tradition in the English novel, as the various uses later made of him by Jane Austen, Thackeray, George Eliot, and Dickens will suggest.

Mimetic prose, then, is not a direct imitation of everyday verbal intercourse but a complex system of equivalences for it, built from literary models and the inventive elaboration of artifice. This system of equivalences usually involves a greater or lesser degree of citation, or pseudocitation, of ordinary language, as I have indicated in juxtaposing texts by Conrad and Gnessin. But there is no general relation between the degree of citation and the force of realistic effect, as one can see from masters of highly wrought style, like Fielding, Flaubert, and Nabokov, who keep citation of the vernacular to a minimum. For more than two centuries novels have been so pervasive in Western culture—and have so often been presented by the writers themselves as "chronicles," "histories," "sagas" of an era, a group, a family, an individual—that we may forget what an unnatural act it is to write a novel. That is, the only way to make a novel work is by a deployment of artifices, both linguistic and narrative; and yet these artifices, when used resourcefully and even cunningly, can give back to us with the illumination of insight our own experience, both as we feel it inwardly and as it is defined through our transactions with others and with the material world.

What this inescapable reliance on literary models of language means is that, in one central regard, the dilemma of the modern

Hebrew writers, however anomalous their linguistic situation, was not unique to them. It may be that every literature at certain points in its evolution needs to create a *nusakh,* as Mendele did in Hebrew, without which it would totter under the weight of inherited stylistic models, producing the effect of literary pastiche rather than the illusion of reality.

The uncertain evolution of fictional prose in nineteenth-century America shows how this problematic of mimesis is shared by literary traditions otherwise radically different from one another. American culture during this period of course had a vigorous colloquial base, but the writers, until fairly late in the century—and for many, even after that—are not willing to trust the vernacular and do not regard it as worthy of literary expression, an uneasiness that goes hand in hand with their frequent feelings of inferiority vis-à-vis the rooted literature of England, the country of cultural origin. Self-conscious about walking on their own American legs, the writers often end up moving stiffly on borrowed literary stilts. The language many of them feel is necessary for the prestige of literary narrative, down to popular writers early in our own century like Jack London and Booth Tarkington, is bombastic and paraphrastic, a compound of formulaic phrases in a diction worlds removed from the vocabulary and cadences of spoken American. It is no less a pastiche than the style of S. Y. Abramowitz before Mendele, though its sources are only occasionally biblical.

Mark Twain provides a famous response to this dilemma of style in *Huckleberry Finn* (1885) by brilliantly installing the American vernacular as the language of narration. But this does not solve the fundamental problem because it works only in the special form of first-person narration—which the Russians call *skaz*—where the author, as a kind of virtuoso ventriloquist, speaks entirely through the persona of a vivid folk narrator whose language is rich in the idiom of the common people. (Hebrew, for lack of a Hebrew-speaking folk, could not do much with *skaz* until recent decades, although it has been an important mode of narration in Yiddish fiction.) It may well be because of the precedent of *Huckleberry Finn* that first-person novels have continued to be favored by American writers down to our own time. But it has been a more complicated business to preserve the poise and control of a third-person narrative, ultimately omniscient, while avoiding literary fustian and while intimating, whether through citation or oblique mimicry, the liveliness of the colloquial language.

In the middle of the nineteenth century, Melville offers an instructive instance of an American genius caught in the toils of pastiche.[2] His prose is often an extraordinary hodgepodge, sometimes wonderful because of his idiosyncratic gifts of invention, sometimes rather awful. The language of *Moby-Dick* is famous for being at many points a mosaic of phrases from Shakespearean tragedy, *Paradise Lost,* and the King James Version of the Bible. Even when there is no direct quotation, there is often a reproduction of the diction and rhythms of seventeenth-century blank verse. Since, reassuringly, there are no ironclad rules in the realm of creativity, Melville does frequently succeed in conjuring up out of these elements of pastiche an authentic poetry of the sublime that quite transcends pastiche. For our purposes, it is more useful to observe his use of language for mimetic rather than poetic ends (though, admittedly, in Melville the two are not fully separable). Here is the initial description of the mysterious stranger who boards the steamboat *Fidèle* in *The Confidence-Man* (1857). It forms the last paragraph of the first chapter:

> Though neither soiled nor slovenly, his cream-colored suit had a tossed look, almost linty, as if traveling night and day from some far country beyond the prairies, he had long been without the solace of a bed. His aspect was at once gentle and jaded, and, from the moment of seating himself, increasing in tired abstraction and dreaminess. Gradually overtaken by slumber, his flaxen head drooped, his whole lamb-like figure relaxed, and, half-reclining against the ladder's foot, lay motionless, as some sugar-snow in March, which softly stealing down over night, with its white placidity startles the brown farmer peering out from his threshold at daybreak.

As a description of an authentic American con-man falling asleep on a riverboat, this is, to say the least, peculiar. Some of the peculiarity may be attributed to the quasi-allegorical impulse of the novel, here ironically associating a figure who will prove to be satanic with the iconography of the snow-white lamb. But, in regard to the arduous task of inventing American prose, the source of peculiarity in the writing is its obtrusive literariness.

The passage begins with an enlivening colloquial touch—"his cream-colored suit had a tossed look, almost linty"—but from then on it is all pastiche. The stranger, in a fabulistic formula, seems to have been "traveling night and day from some far country," with only the specification of "prairies" hinting at an actual American landscape, and further on, we encounter the same locution for fabulous comparison in "some sugar-snow in March." The vernacular "look" of the first sentence is quickly elevated into the more formal "aspect" of the next sentence, a shift in diction already prepared for in the paraphrastic and formulaic epithet for sleep that immediately precedes—"the solace of a bed." By the third sentence, the prose becomes a patchwork of all too familiar poetic phrases—"overtaken by slumber, his flaxen head drooped," "softly stealing down over the night"—that move into the elaboration of a self-conscious Homeric simile: "as some sugar-snow in March, which softly stealing. . . ." The diction is redolent of late eighteenth-century English verse: Akenside, Gray, Cowper, Warton. A small symptom of the excessive distance interposed by literary precedent between the prose and its subject is the "brown" farmer at the end. The epithet is not our ordinary color brown, but an archaic, especially Miltonic use of the term to mean "dusky." Goldsmith writes of the "brown Indian," emphasizing the exoticness of what is for him a remote savage; Melville's brown farmer seems vaguely absurd, a translation of a real farmer into a mere literary locution—like the young Abramowitz's "Hebrews" who, rather than simple Jews, are said to move through the streets of the *shtetl* in his *Fathers and Sons*.

The alternative for mimetic prose to this sort of literary pastiche is not the colloquial language—except in the folkloric performance of *skaz*—but a chastened literary language that eschews antecedent formulas or specialized poetic diction, that lexically, syntactically, and rhythmically suggests the vigor or hominess of the vernacular in the midst of literary artifice. It is only common sense that these vernacular effects should often, in normal linguistic circumstances, arise from a writer's having internalized the actual spoken language. The example of Hebrew, however, argues that a real colloquial base is not strictly necessary: it is enough to have an emphatic downshift in levels of diction, an avoidance of frozen formula, a mining of literary models that sound more like living speech than other literary models.

Let us consider the operation of this dynamic of style in a specimen of American prose a full century after *The Confidence-Man*. Here is a city scene from Saul Bellow's *Herzog* (1964), observed by the protagonist as he leaves a subway station on New York's Upper West Side. The point of my quoting the passage is not, of course, to propose that Bellow is a better writer than Melville, but rather to illustrate how the later novelist benefits from the resources of an established *nusakh* that was not available to the earlier one:

> This was his station, and he ran up the stairs. The revolving gates rattled their multiple bars and ratchets behind them. He hastened by the change booth where a man sat in a light the color of strong tea, and up the two flights of stairs. In the mouth of the exit he stopped to catch his breath. Above him the flowering glass, wired and gray, and Broadway heavy and blue in the dusk, almost tropical; at the foot of the downhill eighties lay the Hudson, as dense as mercury. On the points of radio towers in New Jersey red lights like small hearts beat or tingled. In midstreet, on the benches, old people, on faces, on heads, the strong marks of decay: the big legs of women and blotted eyes of men, sunken mouths and inky nostrils. It was the normal hour for bats swooping raggedly (Ludeyville), or pieces of paper (New York) to remind Herzog of bats. An escaped balloon was fleeing like a sperm, black and quick into the orange dust of the west.[3]

Bellow's writing here illustrates the capacity of realistic prose to give us the world of our experience with a freshness of artistic definition. Anyone who has ever emerged from an I.R.T. station on Broadway in the eighties will recognize the sequence of details precisely observed: turnstile, glass-roofed entrance, the slope down to the Hudson, the radio towers on the other side of the river, the old people on the benches in the concrete traffic island, the scurrying scraps of paper. What concerns us is the character of the language that makes these familiar materials crystallize into a vivid moment of experience.

Because the sequence of perceptions is the character's, up out of the subway and into the sultry street, the language cannot afford to seem pure writerly artifice but must somehow suggest the way such a man would talk to himself. Technically, the passage is a narrated monologue, but this perspective is explicit only when Ludeyville and New York are introduced in parentheses, reminding us that the superimposition of bats on pieces of paper is Herzog's as he collates a recollection of dusk at his Berkshire farmhouse with the present moment in Manhattan. The language bears manifest signs of literary shaping, especially in the luxuriance of metaphoric invention, something that Melville might have appreciated. But in a variety of ways this thoroughly literary language becomes, as I have said, a complex system of equivalences for the vernacular.

Herzog exits through "multiple bars and ratchets," not an ordinary way of designating a turnstile but a defamiliarizing locution that brings to life the metallic reality of the clackety mechanism. "Light the color of strong tea" is as bold a leap of comparison as a head like sugar-snow in March, but the difference between the two is marked by the colloquial compactness and syntactic ease with which the simile is invoked by Bellow. (Imagine the altered effect if, instead of "light the color of . . ." Bellow had written "light that had the peculiar aspect of . . ." or "light of a tincture that seemed like. . . .") Further on, the proliferation of metaphors carries mimetic conviction by virtue of the concision of the images, their anchorage in colloquial terms, their reference to concrete, "subliterary" realia or to the immediacy of kinesthetic sensations: "dense as mercury," "like small hearts beat and tingled," "blotted eyes," "inky nostrils" (a kind of "rhyming" of metaphors), "fleeing like a sperm."

The syntax of the passage is an equally striking illustration of how the use of artifice becomes a simulation of the pulse of experience. "Above him the flowering glass" initiates a sequence of six clauses without predicates (the sole exception, where the subject controls a verb, being "lay the Hudson"). There is nothing very remarkable about this telegraphic style precisely because it is an element of an American *nusakh* that goes back to the 1920s and 1930s, probably influenced by the elliptic syntax of Joyce's stream of consciousness. What I want to stress is that it is patently a literary convention—in fact, we don't ordinarily speak in this fashion without predicates—that conveys the illusion of immediacy of a living inner language: Herzog's internal camera, not pausing for verbs, takes in sequentially the flowering glass overhead, Broadway, the red lights to the west, the benches, the old people, the details of their bodies. Similarly, the syntactical inversions—"glass, wired and gray," "Broadway heavy and blue," "sperm, black and quick"—are violations of vernacular usage in the interests of producing a vernacular effect. That is, they are not poetic inversions, in which normal word order is changed as a matter of literary convention, in keeping with the decorum of a specialized poetic diction, but rather they are notations of the tempo and sequence of the character's perceptions: first he is aware of the object or the place, then of its salient attributes.

If a novelist like Bellow, immersed in the living current of American speech, creates the effect of experiential immediacy chiefly through the resourceful play with artifice (though with an enlivening admixture of elements from the spoken language), it becomes less surprising that a writer like Gnessin, talking and thinking in Russian and Yiddish, should have been able, back at the turn of the century, to produce a similar effect in Hebrew prose. The consonance I noted earlier between Gnessin and other early Hebrew modernists and the latest wave of Israeli fiction throws light on the general problematic of mimesis.

The first native generation of Hebrew fiction—the writers of the 1940s and 1950s—was in part a reversion to pastiche. Either uneasy with or self-conscious about the new colloquial Hebrew (in this respect, resembling the relation of nineteenth-century American writers to their vernacular), these novelists often relied heavily on the verbal formulas of European—especially Russian—fiction as they knew it in Hebrew translation. They also exercised an intermittent, imperfect imitation of Hebrew *nusakh* prose, which sometimes seemed to them the local standard of "fine writing." The writers of the 1970s and 1980s who have brought Hebrew prose to a new level of artistic maturity have been willing to trust the authority of the spoken language to the extent that they feel no need to strain after lofty literary effects. Apart from dialogue, the spoken language is present in their writing through intimation and indirection, through that system of equivalences in artifice we have observed elsewhere. For this reason, their prose at times exhibits intriguing affinities with that of Gnessin and Fogel, though, unlike their European predecessors, they are people whose nursery rhymes and schooling and dreaming were in Hebrew.

A pivotal figure in the latest evolution of Hebrew prose is Yaakov Shabtai, who completed three volumes of fiction (the last published posthumously) before his death in 1981 at the age of forty-seven. His first collection of stories, *Uncle Peretz Takes Off* (*Dod Peretz mamri'*, 1972), is not formally innovative like his two novels, *Past Continuous* (*Zikhron Devarim*, 1977) and *Past Perfect* (*Sof Davar*, 1984), which are bold experiments in interior monologue and the fictional redefinition of time. But even in these early stories, the prose has the air of naturalness of accomplished artifice, with no trace of pastiche or overwrought rhetoric, and with a real power of evocation. I would like to conclude with a passage from Shabtai's title story, not so much to analyze as to illustrate the persuasive force of realized mimesis:

Below, at their feet, lay the sea—gray and brown and tearing
curtains of muddy white. It seethed and noisily hurled its waves
against the desolate shore. The horizon dissolved in the heavy fog,
which kept drawing nearer. The rain became stronger, a direct,
tranquil rain. It fell on the water and on the sand and on the
eroded hills and on the black huts and on the Muslim headstones
and veiled the distant houses, which grew more distant. Everything grew distant and drew near. Uncle Peretz wanted to pick up
his feet and go, but he continued to stand, planted in his place,
and the heavy raindrops fell and washed over his warm face and
momentarily sent through him a light trembling.
"Look how lovely the sea is."[4]

The passage is written in what one might call literary middle
diction. An overt poetic strategy is evident only in the metaphoric activity of the first two sentences—the tearing white curtains of the sea and the more familiar image of seething and
hurling waves. But, in consonance with what we have noted in
Bellow's prose, the most striking effect of immediate observation
is conveyed through a manifest artifice of syntax, the long ana-
phoric chain, "It fell on the water and on the sand. . . ." In the
Hebrew, one feels the implicit presence of an experiential vernacular, but there is scarcely any citation of the vernacular, and as a
token of the continuity with the literary past, there is not a single
word in the passage that would not have been perfectly comprehensible to Gnessin or Mendele. Literary mimesis takes place,
necessarily, through language, but it is not wholly language
because it depends also on the very invention and ordering of
perceptions. Here, one of the qualities of the scene that makes it
so perfectly realized is the peculiar interplay of distance and near-
ness, indicated by the simple verbs *raḥaq* and *qarav,* which is
both an optical effect of the fog and an emotional effect of Uncle
Peretz observing the sea and the landscape. At the heart, then, of
the linguistic artifice is a paradox drawn from experience, not
language, and here given the simplest linguistic translation.
When Uncle Peretz turns to the woman at his side and says,
"Look how lovely the sea is," we as readers stand with him in his

exclamation, feeling the writer has earned it for him by the evocation of this moment of experience.

There is, of course, more to fiction than sheer mimesis, and some kinds of writing may be valued precisely for their anti-mimetic features. But surely one of the primary pleasures of reading is our repeated recognition of the world restored to us with a coherence of definition and inner connection it possesses only rarely in our extraliterary experience of it. Given language's status as an arbitrary code and its entanglement in inherited literary conventions—a predicament that recent literary theorists have repeatedly underscored—it is a wonder that this act of mimetic restoration can take place so often, and so variously. The peculiar story of the fashioning of a realistic prose in Hebrew, because of the very anomaly of the historical circumstances in which it occurred, illumines one aspect of the mystery of mimesis. The success of these writers, working without a vernacular base, reveals something of how language, in all its powerful internal cohesiveness as a formal system evolving through time, may be deployed to evoke the feel and weight and complexity of the real world.

# Notes

## Introduction

1. I make this proposal in the Introduction to my book, *Modern Hebrew Literature* (New York: Behrman House, 1975), p. 2.
2. Ezra Spicehandler, "Hebrew Literature, Modern," in *Encyclopaedia Judaica*, vol. 8 (New York: Macmillan, 1971), p. 182.
3. S. Y. Agnon, *Collected Stories (Kol sipurav shel Shai Agnon)*, vol. 6 (Tel Aviv: Schocken, 1956), p. 252.

## From Pastiche to Nusakh

1. A vivid panorama of this tradition is offered by *The Penguin Book of Hebrew Verse*, ed. T. Carmi (New York: Viking, 1981).
2. Hugh Kenner, "The Politics of Plain Style," in *New York Times Book Review*, 15 September 1985.
3. The classic scholarly account of these two strata is Aba Bendavid, *The Language of the Bible and the Language of the Sages (Leshon Miqra' uleshon ḥakhamim)* (Tel Aviv: Dvir, 1967).
4. I propose a more elaborate account of the cult of the phrase in "Hebrew Literature and the Paradox of Survival," in my book, *After the Tradition* (New York: E. P. Dutton, 1969), pp. 76–92.
5. For an instructive account of some of Abramowitz's strategies of self-translation, see Menakhem Perry, "Analogy and Its Role in Novelistic Structure in Mendele" (*"Ha'anologia umeqomah bemivneh haroman shel Mendele"*), *Ha-Sifrut* 1, no. 1 (Spring 1968): 65–100.
6. Gershon Shaked has commented aptly on the function of balance and synonymity in *Hebrew Fiction: 1880–1970 (Hasiporet ha'ivrit 1880–1970)*, vol. 1 (Tel Aviv: Hakibbutz Hameuchad/Kefer, 1977), p. 88.

## Toward a Language of Experience

1. H. N. Bialik, *Correspondence ('Igrot)*, vol. 2 (Tel Aviv: Dvir, 1938), p. 308.
2. U. N. Gnessin, *Collected Works (Ketavim)*, ed. Dan Miron and Yisrael Zemorah (Tel Aviv: Sifriat Poalim, 1982), p. 141.
3. Erich Auerbach, *Mimesis: The Representation of Reality in Western Literature*, tr. Willard Trask (Princeton: Princeton University Press, 1953), p. 431.
4. It is hard to know whether Gnessin was directly familiar with Henri Bergson, was aware of him by hearsay, or was simply moved by the same *Zeitgeist*. Bergson's pioneering work on time, *Essai sur les données immédiates de la conscience*, appeared in 1889, sixteen years before *To the Side*.

5. Gnessin, *Collected Works,* p. 162.

6. For a full account of both narrated monologue and psycho-narration as narratological categories, see Dorrit Cohn, *Transparent Minds: Narrative Modes for Presenting Consciousness in Fiction* (Princeton: Princeton University Press, 1978), chaps. 1 and 3.

7. Feodor Dostoevsky, *Crime and Punishment,* tr. Jessie Coulson, ed. George Gibian (New York: Norton, 1964), p. 163.

8. I am grateful to Chana Kronfeld for this last observation.

9. Ben Yehudah's historical dictionary of Hebrew, completed just four years after the publication of Gnessin's novella, lists *hakarah* in the sense of "consciousness" as a last meaning, conceding that some modern writers use it this way.

10. On this point, see David Stern, "Midrash and the Language of Exegesis," in *Midrash and Literature,* ed. Geoffrey Hartman and Sanford Budick (New Haven: Yale University Press, 1986).

11. Joseph Conrad, *The Secret Agent* (Garden City: Anchor Books, 1953), p. 58.

12. Gnessin, *Collected Works,* p. 158.

## Realism Without Vernacular

1. Dov Sadan, *Concerning Our Literature (ʿAl Sifruteinu)* (Jerusalem: Reuven Mass, 1950), pp. 10–12.

2. David Fogel, *Facing the Sea (Nokhah hayam)* (Tel Aviv: Siman Keriah, 1974), p. 11.

3. My thanks to Chana Kronfeld for suggesting this possibility.

4. Fogel, *Facing the Sea,* p. 26.

5. Ibid., p. 33.

6. Ibid., p. 70.

7. The word itself (*mistamaʾ*) is an instructive instance of migration from one language to another. Originally an Aramaic term that occurs frequently in the Talmud with a technical-logical meaning ("an inference may be drawn from the general case . . ."), it is adopted in Yiddish to mean, quite conversationally, "apparently," then it returns to Hebrew with its Yiddish force. My thanks to Chana Kronfeld for calling my attention to this point.

8. Fogel, *Facing the Sea,* pp. 50–51.

9. On the stylistic artificiality of the Generation of 1948, see the telling analysis by Gershon Shaked, *A New Wave in Hebrew Fiction (Gal hadash basiporet haʿivrit)* (Tel Aviv: Sifriat Poalim, 1970), pp. 31–41.

## Epilogue: Language and Literary Realism

1. Victor Shklovsky, "A Parodying Novel: Sterne's *Tristam Shandy,*" in *Laurence Sterne,* ed. John Traugott (Englewood Cliffs, N.J.: Prentice-Hall, 1968), p. 89.

2. I owe the idea that Melville illustrates the pastiche-*nusakh* tension to an astute member of the audience at my 1987 Stroum Lectures in Seattle who must, alas, remain anonymous because she did not pause to identify herself.

3. Saul Bellow, *Herzog* (New York: Viking, 1964), p. 178.

4. Yaakov Shabtai, *Uncle Peretz Takes Off* (*Dod Peretz mamri'*) (Tel Aviv: Sifriat Poalim, 1972), p. 157.

# Index

Abramowitz, Shalom Yakov, 24, 102, 113n5; as Mendele the Bookseller, 24, 29–35; *Fathers and Sons,* 24–28; influence of, 67. *See also* Mendele the Bookseller
Agnon, S. Y., 13, 50, 52, 74, 75, 83, 113n3
Allusion: biblical, 23; Haskalah writers' use of, 23–25; relation to *nusakh,* 33–36. *See also Melitsah*
Anaphora, 57. *See also* Repetition
Anti-*nusakh:* origins of, 45–48; in work of Y. H. Brenner, 49–51; in work of Berdichevsky, 46–49
Arabic, 72
Aramaic, 6, 21
*Around the Point (Misaviv lanequdah),* 49–51
Artifice, 19, 94, 100–101, 107
Auerbach, Erich, 55, 113n3
Austen, Jane, 101

Balzac, Honoré de, 23–24
Barthes, Roland, 50
Bellow, Saul, 105–7, 115n2
Bely, Andrey, 40
Bendavid, Aba, 113n3
Ben-Ner, Yitzhak, 61, 79
Ben Yehudah, Eliezer, 114n9
Berdichevsky, Micha Yosef, 46–48, 57, 71, 83, 86, 94
Bergson, Henri, 113n4
Bialik, Haim Nahman, 22, 31, 45–46, 113n1
Bible: study of, 6–9; authority of, 20; allusion to, 23, 33–36; King James Version, 100
Brenner, Yosef Haim, 46, 94; *Around the Point,* 49–50; style of, 50–51, 57; and Zionism, 71

Carmi, T., 113n1
Catalogues: use in *nusakh,* 35–36

Characterization, 92, 103–4; in *nusakh* prose, 32–33; in anti-*nusakh,* 49–51
Chekhov, Anton, 40
Cohn, Dorrit, 59, 114n6
Colloquial. *See* Vernacular
*The Confidence-Man,* 103–5
Conrad, Joseph, 101; *The Secret Agent,* 65–67, 114n11
Consciousness: narratorial rendering of, 40, 48–49, 60, 63, 64–66, 79, 87–88; and temporality, 55–56, 91–92. *See also* Interior monologue; Narrated monologue; Psycho-narration
Convention, 27, 99, 107
*Crime and Punishment,* 59–60
Czaczkes, Shmuel Yosef, 73. *See also* Agnon, S. Y.

Defoe, Daniel, 20, 100
Dialogue: problems of, 24, 25, 64, 78
Dickens, Charles, 27, 33, 40, 101
Diction: in *To the Side,* 61–63; in *Facing the Sea,* 81–83, 92; in American prose, 102–4
Diderot, Denis, 99
*Dod Peretz mamri'. See Uncle Peretz Takes Off*
Dostoevski, Feodor, 50, 59, 114n7

Education: of European Jewry, 6–9, 31
Eliot, George, 50, 101
Erotic experience, fictional representation of, 77–78, 88–89, 91, 92–93

*Facing the Sea (Nokhaḥ hayam),* 77–93
*Fathers and Sons (Ha'avot vehabanim),* 24–28. *See also* Abramowitz, Shalom Yakov

Fielding, Henry, 99, 101
Figurative language, 67, 80; in biblical Hebrew, 27–28; simile, 33; synecdoche, 34, 60, 82; in work of Berdichevsky, 46–48; metaphor, 83, 87–88, 91; in *Herzog*, 106–7
Flaubert, Gustave, 40, 54–55, 64, 88, 99, 101
Fogel, David, 52, 75–76, 94, 108; *Facing the Sea*, 77–82, 114nn 2, 4, 8; ideology of, 83
Free indirect style. *See* Narrated monologue
Freud, Jakob, 4

Generation of 1948, 93, 108, 114n9
Gnessin, Uri Nissan, 45, 46, 49, 51–52, 71, 75, 101, 108, 113nn 2, 4, 114nn 5, 12; *To the Side*, 52–65; temporal transitions in, 53–55; use of rabbinic Hebrew, 64
Gogol, Nikolai, 33
Goldsmith, Oliver, 104
Gordon, Y. L., 12
Gorky, Maxim, 75
Grossman, David, 79

*Ha'avot vehabanim. See Fathers and Sons*
Habimah, 74
Halevi, Judah, 23
Halkin, Simon, 52
HaMe'asef, 4, 11
*HaMe'orer*, 51
*HaShiloah*, 45
Haskalah, 4, 17; prose of, 22; literary aims, 71
*HaTekufah*, 75
*HaTsefirah*, 11
*Hatsidah. See To the Side*
Hawthorne, Nathaniel, 99
*HaYom*, 11
Hazaz, Haim, 35
Hebrew: history of language, 3–9,
18–30, 45–46, 61–62, 63–64, 93–94; role in Jewish culture, 8–9, 12–14, 20, 37–38, 46, 71–72, 94; relation to Yiddish, 10, 12; journalism, 11–12, 45, 51, 74–75; poetry, 18, 76, 88; biblical, 20–21, 22–24, 27, 28, 33–34, 51; rabbinic, 20–22, 30, 36–37, 46, 64, 94, 99; in Palestine, 29, 64; in Italy, 72; in Spain, 72; in Soviet Union, 74–75
*Herzog*, 105–7

Ibn Gabirol, Solomon, 23
Ideology: of early Haskalah, 4, 11; historical role of Hebrew, 13, 71–72; of anti-*nusakh*, 45; transvaluation of Jewish values, 83–84
Idiom: rabbinic Hebrew, 30; European, 37, 47–48; indigenous Hebrew, 37–39, 86
Interior monologue, 108
Irony, 88, 103–4; in biblical allusion, 26

James, Henry, 39, 40
Journalism, Hebrew, 4, 11–12, 45, 74–75
Joyce, James, 64–65, 107

Kafka, Hermann, 4
Kahana-Carmon, Amalia, 52, 61, 79
Kenner, Hugh, 19, 113n2
*Kheyder*, 6, 7

Latin, 20
Lawrence, D. H., 78, 90
Liturgy, 6; allusion to, 25, 30
London, Jack, 102

"*Mahanayim.*" *See* "The Two Camps"
Mailer, Norman, 93, 100
Mann, Thomas, 78
Mapu, Avraham, 24

*Melitsah,* 23–24, 26. *See also* Allusion
Melville, Herman, 103–4, 115n2
Memory, 60–61, 62
Mendele the Bookseller, 29–40, 45, 57, 64, 67, 71, 94, 113n5. *See also* Abramowitz, Shalom Yakov; *Nusakh*
Mendelssohn, Moses, 17
Metaphor. *See* Figurative language
Midrash, 21, 30, 58, 63
Migration: of Hebrew movement, 4; to Palestine, 73; to West, 73–74
*Mimesis,* 55
Mimesis, 94, 100–101, 108–10
*Misaviv lanequdah. See Around the Point*
Mishnah, 7, 21, 30, 58, 63
Modernism, early Hebrew, 52–63
Mokher Sefarim, Mendele, 6. *See also* Mendele the Bookseller
Multilingualism, 72–73; in work of Berdichevsky, 46–48

Nabokov, Vladimir, 78, 101
Narrated monologue, 48, 55, 58, 66, 91
Narration, 40, 48–49, 66, 78–80, 84–85, 87–88, 91–92
Narrator: in *Facing the Sea,* 84–85; in *Huckleberry Finn,* 102–3
Neologism, 63
*Nokhah hayam. See Facing the Sea*
Novel: relation to realism, 4–5; eighteenth-century English, 19, 100–101; conventions of, 27–28, 99; generic style, 39–40, 100–101; Russian, 40, 59–60, 108; twentieth-century European, 77–78; objects of representation in, 85–86; relation to spoken language, 99–100, 108; conceptual procedures of, 99–102; and autobiography, 100–101; American, 102–7

*Nusakh,* 102, 105; definition of, 31–32; example of, 32–33; and allusion, 33–36; and use of idiom, 37–38; limitations of, 40; resistance to, 45–47; influence of, 57–58. *See also* Anti-*nusakh*

Pagis, Dan, 76
Parataxis, 21. *See also* Syntax
Pastiche, 24, 103–4, 108
Pathos, 28–29, 34–35
Perry, Menakhem, 113n5
Poetry, Hebrew, 18, 76
Premodern tradition: in Hebrew literature, 3–4, 18–19
Proletariat, urban Jewish, 10
Psycho-narration, 59, 66, 91–92

Realism, 19, 84–85, 99; psychological, 17, 91–92; and spoken language, 19; descriptive, 29–30, 35–36, 105–7; experiential, 40–41, 57, 64–65, 109–10; social, 40; satiric, 100–101
Repetition: in fictional narrative, 54; affective, 56–57
Richardson, Samuel, 20, 100

Sadan, Dov, 71, 73, 114n1
Satire, 32–33
Schneour, Zalman, 45
Schocken, Zalman, 74, 75
*The Secret Agent,* 65–66
Shabtai, Yaakov, 79, 108–10, 115n4
Shaked, Gershon, 113n6, 114n9
"Shem and Japheth on the Train" (*"Shem vaYefet ba'agalah"*), 32–36, 38–39
*"Shem vaYefet ba'agalah." See* "Shem and Japheth on the Train"
Shklovsky, Victor, 99, 114n1
Simile. *See* Figurative language
*Skaz,* 102

Social class: traditional Eastern European Jewry, 6; of Hebrew writers, 9–11; and the English novel, 19
Soviet revolution: effect on Hebrew literature, 74–75
Spain, 72
Spicehandler, Ezra, 9, 113n2
Sprat, Bishop Thomas, 19
Steinberg, Yakov, 45
Stendhal, 39, 64
Stern, David, 114n10
Sterne, Laurence, 50, 100; *Tristram Shandy*, 99, 100–107
Stream of consciousness, 101
Stybel, 75
Style: in early Hebrew novel, 17, 24–28; biblical Hebrew, 21–22; rabbinic Hebrew, 21–22, 28–29; transformation of Hebrew prose, 29–38; novelistic, 50–51, 90–91; in eighteenth-century English novel, 100–101; in *The Confidence-Man*, 103–4. *See also Nusakh* and Anti-*nusakh*
*Style indirect libre*. *See* Narrated monologue
Subjects: of early Hebrew fiction, 10, 29, 45; of early Hebrew modernism, 52–53, 77, 79
Synecdoche. *See* Figurative language
Synonymity, 22, 35–36
Syntax: biblical, 21; rabbinic, 21; in "The Two Camps," 48; in *Around the Point*, 49–50; in *Herzog*, 107; in *Uncle Peretz Takes Off*, 109

Talmud, 7
Tarkington, Booth, 102
Tchernichovsky, Saul, 45

Tenses: biblical Hebrew, 21, 51, 85; rabbinic Hebrew, 21, 27; in work of Uri Gnessin, 53–55, 62; and fictional representation of time, 54–55
Thackeray, William Makepeace, 101
Time, fictional representation of, 53–56, 108
*To the Side* (*Hatsidah*), 52–59, 61
Tolstoi, Lev Nikolayevich, 40
Twain, Mark, 102–3
Twersky, Yokhanan, 45
"The Two Camps," ("*Mahanayim*"), 47–49

*Uncle Peretz Takes Off* (*Dod Peretz Mamri'*), 108–10
United States: emigré Hebraists in, 73

Vernacular, 29, 64, 66–67, 100–101, 102, 106. *See also Skaz*
Vernacular-like, 57–58, 64, 99, 106–7
Vocabulary: in biblical Hebrew, 21; in rabbinic Hebrew, 22, 30; expansion of, 62, 86. *See also* Diction
Von Dohm, Christian Wilhelm, 3

Yehoshua, A. B., 61, 79
*Yeshivah*, 7–8
Yiddish: education, 6–7; and Jewish proletariat, 10; relation to Hebrew, 12, 17; novel, 24. *See also* Vernacular
Yizhar, S., 52, 61

Zionism, 12, 15, 71; second Aliyah, 73; effect on Hebrew literature, 74